AFRICAN INFLUENCE IN THE UNITED NATIONS, 1967 - 1975:

The Politics and Techniques of
Gaining Compliance to U.N.
Principles and Resolutions

Gregory L. Wilkins
Shaw College at Detroit

University Press
of America™

Copyright © 1981 by
University Press of America, Inc.™
P.O. Box 19101, Washington, DC 20036

ISBN: 0-8191-1425-1 Perfect
0-8191-1424-3 Case
Library of Congress Number: 80-5734

#71.973

PREFACE

This research grew out of a general interest in the nature and process of "influence" in the international political system. The previous work done in influence revealed that political scientists tend to suggest that "influence" occurred only and when a desired outcome resulted.

However, this study was more interested in understanding "influence" as a process in the United Nations. In other words the concern was to answer two broader questions: How do nations attempt to gain compliance to U.N. principles and resolutions among each other? What specific strategies are employed by nations to gain compliance?

To determine this we sought to identify a particular bloc of nations, the African nations, in the U.N. who desored to gain compliance to certain U.N. principles and resolutions in an attempt to resolve world issues that were of paramount concern to them. By incorporating the case study method of the particular issues we attempt to reveal whether there are specific strategies that African nations in particular and perhaps nations in general use to gain compliance to international principles and resolutions.

A final focus of the study was to gain insight into the nature and behavior of African nations as a bloc in the United Nations. In other words do these nations act cohesively in an attempt to gain compliance to those U.N. principles and resolutions relevant to the issues of greatest blocs of African nations themselves in terms of favoring certain strategies for gaining compliance to U.N. principles and resolutions relevant to the issues of greatest concern to the African bloc? Is there variation among the various blocs of African nations themselves in terms of favoring certain strategies for gaining compliance to U.N. principles and resolutions. In other words do some African nations tned to favor more militant or conciliatory strategies of influence than others on various issues?

It is hoped that this study will give greater insight ' into the nature of "influence" in the international political system, bloc politics in the U.N., and African politics in the international system.

Dedicated to the loving memory of
my maternal grandmother,
Mrs. Dicie Powers

ACKNOWLEDGEMENTS

I would like to express gratitude to all those individuals who contributed in some way to my successfully completing this project. I must give special
thanks to Professor Bernice Carroll of the Department
of Political Science of the University of Illinois at
Urbana, for their invaluable comments and suggestions made
with respect to the manuscript. Also, I must give special
thanks to my mother and sisters, Carol and Marjorie, for
their unrelenting support and encouragement during the com-
pletion of this project. Finally, I received support from
a number of friends and colleagues, Ella Bowen, Oscar Draper,
Marilyn M. Goings, Margaret Royal, Kathy Royal, Frederick Salsman,

TABLE OF CONTENTS

Page

TABLE OF CONTENTS (Continued)

LIST OF TABLES

LIST OF TABLES

Page

CHAPTER I

INTRODUCTION

The decade of the 1960's witnessed the creation of
numerous, independent African nations freed from their
former colonial status. Thus, African peoples assumed
a new status in the international community. One of
the first things most of these nations did as sovereign
entities was to obtain membership in the United Nations.

African nations must have been a significant force in
the United Nations since 1963. (see Table I) By that
year some 33 newly independent African nations had joined
the international community of the United Nations, coming
to represent one-third of the total membership of the
United Nations. The political significance of this ermergence
of Africa in the United Nations is suggested by David Kay's
observation on its earlier composition:

> The United Nations has been created primarily
> through the efforts of states with a European
> or European derived political and social culture,
> possessing a common history of political involve-
> ment at the international level. During its first
> ten years the Organization was dominated by the
> problems and conflicts of these same states.[1]

Implicit in Kay's observation is the idea that an increments
ment in the membership of the United Nations from nations of a
different political and social culture might alter the political
system of the United Nations.

Because participation in the world organization was a
novel experience for most African nations, in 1963 they began
with limited knowledge of how to maximize their gains in the
political process of the international community. "As a
result of the sudden and unexpected nautre of their entry
into the organization, the African states shared a general
deficiency of the skilled individuals and resources necessary
for full participation in international diplomacy.[2] We have
therefore, chosen a later year, 1967, as a more appropriate
point of departure for a study of how African nations
function in the United Nations. By 1967, the formal process

TABLE I

YEAR OF ENTRY OF AFRICAN
NATIONS INTO THE UNITED NATIONS

1945 - 1949

Egypt
Ethiopia
Liberia

1950 - 1959

Ghana
Guinea
Morocco
Sudan
Tunisia

1960 - 1964

Algeria
Burundi
Cameroon
Central African Republic
Chad
Congo (Brazzaville)
Congo (Leopoldville)
Dahomey
Gabon
Ivory Coast
Kenya
Madagascar
Malawi
Mali
Mauritania
Niger
Nigeria
Rwanda
Sierra Leone
Senegal
Somali Republic [Samalia]
Tanzania
Togo
Upper Volta
Uganda
Zanzibar
Zambia

TABLE I (Continued)

1965 - 1969

Botswana
Equatorial Guinea
Gambia
Lesotho
Swaziland

1970 - 1975

Democratic Republic of Sao Tome & Principe
Guinea Bissau
People's Republic of Mozambique
Republic of Cape Verde

of "decolonization" was over for most of the African
nations. (38 by the end of the year) Moreover, many
of these nations had had time in which to establish,
acclimate and familiarize themselves with the United
Nations organization and its politics. By 1967, the
African nations have had an opportunity to establish
descernible patterns of behavior in the political
process of the United Nations.

A review of the literature of the work on the
United Nations and Africa reveals two main groups of
studies.

The first group tended to concentrate on predicting
that future importance and impact the United Nations
would have on African problems when African nations began
emerging as independent nations and joining the United
Nations. A preponderance of works was written about this
time period, 1959 and the 1960's. A work such as
Sir Andrew Cohen's "The New Africa and the United Nations"
seeks to identify factors that go to ensure that African
nations will be highly influential in the United Nations
after 1960,aand what issues shall be of paramount concern
to these nations in the United Nations. Cohen's thesis
is that African nations will be quite influential because
they work more closely together than any other group except the Soviet bloc, and because of the wide sympathy for
African aspirations felt in all sections of the United
Nations and their association with the Afro-Asian bloc.
As to the issues of concern to African nations in the
United Nations, Cohen predicts three as being paramount:
Cold War Conflict, racial issues,aand under development.[3]

Irvine Keith's article, "African Nationalism and the
U.N.", offers the same type of analysis and conclusion as
Cohen except that he adds that African nations have a profound hope in the U.N. as a vehicle which will play an
important role in their advancement.[4]

Joan Gillespie's article "Africa's Voice at the United
Nations," written in 1959, identifies and describes the cohesion of African nations in the U.N. and points out that it
differed from other blocs in that it did not develop to deal
with specific issues at the U.N.

-4-

She further points out that the other primary con-
tributing factor to African cohesion was the fact
that African nations began to see their interests as
more distinct from those of the larger Afro-Asian
Bloc.[5]

The second group of scholarly works on Africa in
the United Nations tends to study voting patterns and
make inferences based on those patterns. These works
primarily concern themselves with validating a single
thesis that African nations in the U.N. form a distinct
bloc which is based upon solidarity of votes on various
issues that come before the U.N. Some works that represent this dimension of Africa in the United Nations are:
Will Maslow's "The Afro-Asian Bloc in the United Nations,"[6]
Thomas Hovet's Bloc Politics In The United Nations,[7] and
Vernon McKay's Africa In World Politics.[8]

There are several works which have a more direct
relationship to our concerns with respect to African
nations in the United Nations.

The first of these is Moses E. Akpan's African Goals
and Diplomatic Strategies In The United Nations.[9] Akpan's
study which focuses upon 1960-1974, asserts that the three
primary goals of African nations in the United Nations were:
(1) political freedom for Africa, seeking to achieve the
total independence from colonial and settler rule; 2)
elimination of racial discrimination from Africa; (3) economic and technical assistance for their economic progress.
Akpan then uses three case studies to analyze the diplomatic
strategies African nations in the United Nations employ
to realize these goals. He uses the case studies of South
West Africa, South-Africa, and the establishment of the
African Development Bank and the Institute For Economic
Development and Planning for his analysis.

While Akpan's stated purpose was to identify African
diplomatic strategies for achieving their goals in the
U.N., his study does not document in a specific and hard
fast fashion the detailed strategies that African nations

exclusively employed in the U.N. to realize their
goals. What he does document is merely the proposals
either supported by or initiated by African nations in
the U.N. which were consistent with their goals as he
defined them. Akpan concludes in his work that because
of a lack of military and material power to achieve
independently their own goals in world affairs, African
nations have turned to the United Nations with little
substantive results other than the mere passage of non-
enforced resolutions.

The second notable work is Thomas Hovet's Africa
in the United Nations. This work, published in 1963,
is primarily concerned with determining the forms and
degree of cohesian or cooperativeness that African
nations have developed in the United Nations. The most
important is that African nations in the United Nations
do or attempt to function cohesively or cooperatively.
Hovet traces in detail the development of African cooperation in the United Nations.

At the creation of the United Nations in 1945,
Africa had no political identity in the organization.
Although Egypt, South Africa, Ethiopia, and Liberia were
participants in the San Francisco conference and original
members of the United Nations, they did not contribute to
an identity of African interests to the organization.[10]
Egypt was allied in the Organization more with the interests
of the Middle Eastern nations and the Arab League. South
Africa cooperated with and organized around issues in
the United Nations with the British Commonwealth group
since she was a self-governing dominion of Britain. Ethiopia
and Liberia functioned in an isolated manner in the United
Nations because never having been colonies (except when
Ethiopia was occupied by Italian forces), they symbolized
little of the aspirations for self-government and independence
that were just beginning to stir in the rest of the African
colonies.[11]

But, two subsequent events were to prove crucial in
changing this situation of Africa in the United Nations.
As a result of the Bandung Conference of Asian and African
States and the Conference of Independent States at Accra, an
African presence in the United Nations was created. In other
words, it was as a result of these two conferences that the
formal basis of African cooperation in the United Nations
was established.

The Bandung Conference was a conference of Asian and
African states from April 18-24, 1955. This conference
was summoned by the prime ministers of several Asian
countries. The primary purpose of the conference was
to promote and establish cooperation between African
and Asian nations by considering and exploring mutual
and common interests and considering problems of particular interests to Asian and African peoples. The Bandung
Conference convened representatives of the African states,
Egypt, Gold Coast, Ethiopia, Liberia and the Sudan with
Eighteen Asian nations to define issues of vital concern
to their interest.

This development was consolidated three years later
when the Conference of Independent African States was held in
Accra, April 15-22, 1958. This conference of the
attending states of Ethiopia, Libya, Ghana, Morocco,
Sudan, Tunisia, and United Arab Republic, discussed problems
and issues of mutual interests. "The Accra Conference built
a road for Africa in world affairs and in the United Nations
which had inspired its deliberations."[12] The road that the
Accra Conference created for Africa in the United Nations was
clearly defined in the resolutions that the conference passed,
formally establishing African cooperation or cohesion in the
United Nations. "It will be recalled that Resolution XI of
the Accra Conference provided that the permanent representatives of the African nations to the United Nations would constitute themselves as a working group for coordinating matters
of common concern."[13] Thus, the permanent representatives of
the African nations to the United Nations met and established
by a formal agreement an African caucusing group in the United
Nations. By 1962, the Caucus consisted of 32 members. The
African caucus is one of the largest in the United Nations.

In Africa and International Organization, edited by
Yassin El-Ayouty and Hugh C. Brooks,[14] an assessment of the
impact of Africa on the U.N. and the relationship between the
OAU and U.N. is made.

In this volume it is observed by Thomas Hovet in the
article "The Effect of the African Group of States on The

7

Behavior of the United Nations," that the presence of African states in the U.N. the organization has increased its interest in the troubles of the continent. Two-thirds of the business of the U.N. within the last decade has been concerned with economic and social development and the achievement of self-determination.

The emphasis of the U.N. during the first decade was primarily peace maintenance rather than focusing on the cause of conflict. Since the influx of the African states the U.N.'s focus has been on the causes of conflict.

African presence in the U.N. has brought changes in the structured roles of the organization because the African states have demanded a representative voice in the organization. As a result, through formal amendment of the U.N. Charter, key bodies of the U.N. have enlarged their membership, e.g., the Security Council and the Economic and Social Council.

With respect to the relationship between the OAU and the U.N. it is observed by James O.C. Jonah in his article "the U.N. and the O.A.U.," that of all regional organizations, the O.A.U. has the closest links with the United Nations and its subsidiary organs. This cooperation has been primarily in the economic, technical, social and administrative fields. The O.A.U. has achieved observer status within the United Nations and had built its link through participation in the Economic Commission of Africa, Economic and Social Council, and the Special Committee on the Policies of Apartheid of the Government of South Africa.

A fourth source of theoritical foundation for our study is to be found in the work of David Kay, The New Nations In The United Nations. Although this is not exclusively concerned with African nations, they are included within the broader socpe of the work.

Kay, in his study, examines the political process of the United Nations during the period of 1960-67 "... from the perspective of the demands made by the new nations on the Organization and the political influence they have wielded in attempting to advance these demands."15 Thus, Kay seeks to define the nature of the demands placed on the United Nations political process from the new nations of Africa, Asia, the Americas, Europe, and the Middle East and to measure the degree of their influence on that process as it relates to those demands.

Since African nations were a chief component in Kay's study it may be of interest to compare the issues raised by African nations before the U.N. during the period with which we are concerned, (1967 and 1975) with those that Kay found to be important for all new nations during the period of 1960-67. Kay's data reveal that the interests of and demands placed before the U.N. by the new nations were essentially two: decolonization and economic aid and development. Thus, we will be interested in noting whether this pattern has changed in the case of the African nations during the period of 1967-75.

While Kay is aware of the fact that is is one thing to get resolutions passed in the U.N. and an altogether different matter to gain compliance to these resolutions from member nations in the United Nations, his study of "influence" was confined to the former aspect. In this study we will focus upon the types of actions favored by African nations as strategies to gain compliance by other nations to those resolutions and principles of the United Nations with which they are highly concerned.

Thus, our study will differ from Kay's in geographical scope, period of focus, and conceptual framework. These differences will become clearer as we discuss the specific design of our proposed research.

Influence: An Analytical Framework

"Influence" like other abstract concepts in the
social sciences presents a formidable problem of definition.
Political scientists and other social scientists have
defined it in a variety of ways.

"Influence" has been defined in terms of "effect
on outcome". In accord with this definition a state
or actor is influential in the United Nations insofar as
it is able to affect the decisions of the General
Assembly membership so that they accord with its wishes.
This conception of "influence" would dictate that "influence"
be measured simply by compiling the percentage of times
a state or member of the United Nations votes with the
majority of the group. The greater a state's majority-
support score, the more influential it will be considered.

This quanitative orientation and approach to determining "influence" was further developed by L.S. Shapely
and Martin Shubik. These social scientists favor measuring
"influence" in decision-making bodies or committees by
compiling "influence" "ratings".... by comparing the probability that an actor was 'pivotal' on any given series of
votes with his a prior probability of being 'pivotal'.[16]
"Thus, in a nine-member committee each member has a hypo-
thetical influence value of 1/9; however on a decision
taken by a 5-4 majority; each majority member is assigned
an influence value of 1/5 (that is 1/n, where n is the
number of the minority is assigned a value of zero."[17]

The other mathematical model of measuring "influence"
in the United Nations Assembly is the "legislative-effec-
tiveness" concept introduced by Donald Matthews. This
model determines the degree of "influence" by measuring
". . . the proportion of resolutions introduced by an actor
that are passed by the legislative body."[18]

Mathematical models are not accurate and useful tools
for measuring "influence" when you are interested as
we are in examining it as a process. As Robert Keohane
argues, "The common problem with the legislative-effec-
tiveness and majority-support tests is that one must
infer the extent of a state's influence from the
results of Assembly action with no way of determining
the impact of that particular state on those results."[19]
In this framework, the dynamics of the process of influence,
which may or may not result in output, is not analyzed to
any great extent.

In this study, we qualify our definition and conception of "influence" by conceptualizing it as a process,
the strategies (including the political tactics) used
or favored to gain compliance or adherence to U.N.
principles and resolutions from nations in the U.N.

By examining systematically the U.N. general debate
speeches of African nations, we can identify the political
actions and recommendations expressly favored by African
nations to gain compliance or adherence to U.N. principles
and resolutions. While our systematic study here is limited
to the general debate speeches, we also take note of historical background and some foreign policy actions taken
outside of the United Nations, especially those which relate
directly to the recommendations favored by African nations
in the U.N. General Debate. This may help us to assess
whether those recommendations take the form of real action
in the international system and are thereby indicative of
some ongoing process of influence.

This is an even more appropriate approach in view of an
important feature of the U.N. Assembly political system:
compliance to resolutions of the United Nations assembly is
not obligatory upon the part of member nations. As the history
of the United Nations shows resolutions which have been passed
by the Assembly commonly fail to gain compliance from many
member nations. Thus, nations have had to resort to techniques

and strategies of influencing a nations behavior
even after an initial resolution designed to resolve
a particular issue has been passed.

In a systematic analysis of the implementation
of decisions of the United Nations on the study of some
313 resolutions passed by the United Nations General Assembly
Catherine Manno, reached some relevant conclusions for
our study. The first and foremost conclusio· was that
the largest category of decisions passed by the United Nations
General Assembly were "internal decisions". Internal decisions
are the means by which the Assembly organizes itself and guides
and budgets the activities of its own subsidiary organs, the
Secretariat, and other organs and agencies insofar as
they come under its jurisdiction.[20] This category of decisions
consituted more than half of all resolutions requiring implemen-
mentation. "While there is no problem of getting internal
decisions implemented, the situation is quite different with
recommendatory decisions."[21] The former type of resolutions
encounter no difficulty in being implemented because they
are not dependent directly on individual states for compliance.
Secondly, the category of decisions which encounter difficulty
in compliance are those Assembly recommendatory resolutions.
The following was observed about his type of United Nations
Decision:

> Even though directed to all members, Assembly
> recommendations seldom have equal impact
> on all. However, small the scale, a re-
> distributive process is usually involved.
> This differential nature of decisions is
> more marked in the next category. . .,
> recommendations mainly dependent for
> compliance on a particular subgroup of
> members...[22]

Therefore, Manno's work substantiates the fact that
resolutions passed by the U.N., which do not relate to internal organizational matters, experience difficulty in being
implemented by the U.N. member nations.

The United Nations' Political System

To help understand allusions to different organs of the United Nations throughout this study it is necessary here to summarize the formal and informal decision-making structure of the U.N. body itself.

The structure of power and decision-making of the United Nations created by the charter was based on two assumptions: (1) the primary function of the Organization was to preserve international peace and security; (2) the nations possessed with the most highly capable weapons in the world should have a special responsiblity in making decisions about the maintenance of international peace and security; the nations possessed with the most highly capable weapons in the world should have a special responsibility in making decisions about the maintenance of international peace and security. Thus, to realize the goals of the U.N. based on these assumptions, the organization established these principal organs: The Security Council General Assembly , Economic and Social Council, Trusteeship Council, International Court of Justice, and the Secretariat. In terms of power and the authority to make decisions for the United Nations Organizations,the principle organs involved in the decision making process are the Security Council, General Assembly, and the International Court of Justice.

The Security Council's authority as defined by the charter is rather extensive, particularly as compared with the other organs of the United Nations' political process. The Security Council is the only organ of the United Nations whose decisions are binding upon the member nations. In addition, the Security Council has exclusive power in the area of security problems confronting the international community. The nature of the power of the Security Council is succinctly noted as one scholar of the United Nations observes:

> The Charter empowered the Security
> Council to recommend means of peaceful
> settlement of disputes; and, if a nation
> committed an act of aggresion, the Council
> was to have the power to apply sanctions
> against the aggresor. Such sanctions might

range from the severance of diplomatic
relations all the way to collective
military action.23

The Security Council's membership is limited by the
charter to fifteen member nations, five of which are permanent: United States, Russia, United Kingdom, France, and
China. The remaining members are elected for two-year terms.
"The nations at San Francisco were agreed that any system
created for keeping the peace after WW II must include all
the major powers, and particularly the United States and
the Soviet Union, the two nations that would have the
greatest military potential at the end of the war. ..."24
The security council can make no substantive decision
without the unanimous vote of the five permanent members.
Thus, the extensive nature of the Security Council's
power in the United Nations is related to its formal right
to make binding decisions, decisions related to security
and collective security measures.

The formal structure of power of the General Assembly
body offers a striking contrast. The United Nations General
Assembly is duly ". . . granted the authority to discuss '
any questions or any matters within the scope of the present
charter or relating to the powers and functions of any organ
provided for in the present charter and . . . may make recommendations to the   members of the United Nations or to the
Security Council or both or any such questions or matters.'25

Thus, the General Assembly is not formally a legislative body. The resolutions passed by the Assembly are not
binding upon member nations but are only recommendatory.
Therefore, the General Assembly is empowered to pass resolutions
on the wide range of principles to which the United Nations
is dedicated. The General Assembly may pass resolutions on
issues related to international cooperation in the political
economic, social, and human rights field.

Membership in the General Assembly body is not limited.
In fact, it is the only organ of the United Nations in which all
member nations participate. It is the body in which all
nations, regardless of size or military capability, can offer

a resolution, debate an issue, and indulge in diplomacy or raise any issue it feels confronts the international community.

The Informal Structure of Power of United Nation's Political System

In assessing the "informal" authority in the United Nations' political system, the primary focus is upon the General Assembly, This body has assumed far greater "Informal authority than the other two organs, the Security Council, and the International Court of Justice. Although "formally" the area of decisions it can make is restricted and its decisions are not binding, the Assembly has come to be the supreme body of the United Nations. Because it has transcended its "formal" role as merely a "creative body" -- creative in the sense that is its function, exclusively,".. the formulation of principles to promote peaceful adjustments and friendly relations among nations "26 --the General Assembly has become supreme in the United Nations' political system. In striking contrast the Security Council was concieved as the 'organ of action': shouldering the responsibility for taking enforcement action in the case of an act of aggression in the world. The transcendence of authority by the Aoocmbly has come about as a response to world politics in the post World War II era. Now the Assembly serves as a creative as well as an active function. "The profound disagreements that arose between the great powers after the adoption of the Charter led increasingly to deadlock in the Security Council and to use of the Assembly for initiating action to advance the Charter's aims, and a gradual breakdown of the lines of functional separation between the two organs followed."27

The "authority" and function of the Assembly have altered with time. For example, in response to the inability of the Security Council to deal with the Korean problem after August 1950, the Assembly transcended its formal authority to peacekeeping problems by sanctioning and approving collective enforcement measures. In the "Uniting for Peace" resolutions the Assembly established its right to recommend the use of collective military measures by "stressing the Assembly's residual responsibility for maintaining peace."28 The United

Nations Assembly:

> ...resolved that if the Council is
> prevented by the veto from discharging
> primary responsibility in the security
> field when a threat to the peace, breach
> of the peace, or act of aggression occurs,
> the Assembly itself 'shall consider the
> matter immediately with a view to making
> appropriate recommendations to members for
> collective measures, including in the
> case of a breach of the peace or act of
> agression the use of armed forces when
> necessary to maintain or restore international
> peace and security.[29]

The importance of the authority of the Assembly is
heightened by the fact that the more pressing and critical
issues confronting the world have been handled by this
body e.g., international control of nuclear weapons, the
promotion of political, economic, and social development,
the termination of colonialism. "Many member governments
have come to perceive the Assembly as a more suitable body
than the Council to foster their interests."[30] Thus, the
General Assembly has assumed an importance far greater
than that envisioned by the San Francisco Conference.

"Assembly resolutions, moreover, while technically only
recommendations, have been viewed by several Member Countries,
with regard to certain matters and within certain limits, as
legally binding decisions."[31] Those resolutions which
facilitate the principles of the United Nations are considered by legalists to be binding upon member nations. The
real "legal status" of resolutions of the United Nations'
Assembly is an unresolved issue among legalists. It is however, safe to assume that nations that participate in the
United Nations Assembly deliberations attach a seriousness to
its decisions also.

The General Assembly, although not the parliament that
it resembles... has greatly expanded its activities, sometimes
through intent, at other times through the accident of the
failure of certain organs of the United Nations (especially
the Security Council) to function as expected.[32] The

importance of the Assembly is attested to by the fact
that it"... has become both the political pivot and
the institutional pith of the entire United Nations
system." [32]

The General Assembly has superseded the role it
was envisioned to play by the architects of the Charter
of the United Nations. "Individual members have more and
more come to place reliance upon the Assembly, which is,
in the last analysis, the supreme supervisory body of
the United Nations." [34]

"Influence", African Nations, and the United Nations

In order that we can draw clear hypotheses about
African "influence" in the United Nations, we must
synthesize an operation definition of "influence" (see
below) with an understanding of the political process
of the United Nations' system. Our premises can be
summarized as follows:

African Nations

The term "African Nations" as used in this work
refers to all nations that hold membership in the Organization of African Unity. This explicitly excludes the
white-dominated regimes of outhern Africa, South Africa,
South West Africa and Rhodesia. Sometimes it will be
necessary to refer to these nations, which are geographical-
ly on the continent of Africa, as "African"; but in general
our usage includes only the independent, non-white dominated states.

The United Nations' Political System

The basic unit of the political system is the nation
state. All nation-states of the United Nations belong to
and interact in the General Assembly body. The United
Nations General Assembly decisions can affect the interests
of a nation state. Because General Assembly resolutions are
not binding upon member states, additional techniques of
"influence" are often employed.

-17-

"Influence"

"Influence," is here defined as a process of working to gain compliance to the principles and resolutions of the United Nations.

As a result of the unique features of the United Nations' political system, African nations, in order to exercise "influence," have come to form and act as a subsystem within the United Nations and the international system. In contending that African nations act as a subsystem" within the United Nations we are referring to their pattern of relations and interaction with each other and with the other members of the United Nations. This pattern of relations between African nations must be under - stood within the global or world system as represented by the United Nations, which it seeks to affect.

According to "system" theorists in international relations, there exist three systems or patterns of inter- action between nation states: (1) World or Global System, (2) Dominant System, (3) Subordinate System. The World or Global System constitutes the total web of relation- ships among all actors within the international system. The Dominant System involves the interaction between the superpowers of the world. The latter, the Sub- ordinate system, the one relevant to African nations in the United Nations, "...represents an intermediate level of interaction between the global system and the relations between any two states."[35]

Subordinate Systems can be classified accordingly: (1) geographic, with contiguous membership; (2) geographic, with non-contiguous members; (3) organizational, with con- tiguous membership; and (4) organizational, with non-con- tiguous members. "The concept of Subordinate State System is more rigorous and requires six conditions: (1) its scope is delimited, with primary stress on a geographic region; (2) there are at least three actors; (3) taken together, they are objectively recognized by other actors as con- stituting a distinctive community, region, or segment of the Global System; (4) the members themselves identify themselves as such; (5) the units of power are relatively inferior to units in the Dominant System, using a sliding scale of power in both; and (6) changes in the Dominant

System have greater effect on the Subordinate System than the reverse."[36] These criteria apply to the OAU.

In discussing African nations' influence, the importance of the OAU as a pivot of African cooperation in international politics must be emphasized. The organization, created in 1963, brought together 31 independent African nations into an international organization named the Organization of African Unity to address itself to international issues of common concern to all African states, including those in the international sphere. Not surprisingly, the same issues which were of concern to African nations in the OAU were also major issues of concern in the United Nations. Thus, the OAU complemented and fostered coordination of African efforts on international issues in the United Nations.

All of the literature reviewed on Africa in the United Nations supports strongly the idea that African nations are cohesive in the U.N. body. However, the indices of cohesion in supporting this argument have been primarily voting patterns of Arican nations in the U.N.

Since the study here consists of a systematic study of the speeches of African nations in the U.N. General Debate, our index of cohesion is different. Our study cannot assume that African nations in the U.N. are cohesive but must reserve such determination since our index will be based upon the recommendations and political actions favored on the issues discussed in their U.N. Debate Speeches. The examination of speeches may be more interesting in assessing cohesion because it permits systematic consideration of every individual nation's expression whereas votes as a measure of cohesion merely reflect majority positions.

In order that our analysis be thorough we must allow for the fact that there may exist variation among African nations in terms of predilections for the use of certain types of techniques on the various issues of concern in the United Nations. We,therefore,consider such questions as: Do some groups of African nations favor harsher tactics of influence to gain compliance to United Nations resolutions and

principles than others? Do those groups of African
nations who favor the harsher techniques of influence tend
to be more vociferous, i.e. to speak more frequently on
issues, than others?

Our research seeks to examine the following hypotheses:

(1) African nations in the United Nations show
discernible, consistent patterns or strategies
in their recommendations of techniques for
gaining compliance to those United Nations
resolutions and principles that relate to the
issues of greatest concern to them.

(2) There exists variation amoung groups of
African nations which tend to prefer the use
of one particular strategy of influence more
than another on various issues in gaining
compliance to United Nations' principles and
resolutions.

Variation will be analyzed in the following chapters
along geographical lines. It is customary in some of the
literature on African states to treat them by geographical
division -- e.g., West Africa, East Africa, etc. The geographical groupings of African Nations are Central Africa,
East Africa, North Africa, Southern Africa (black majority
regions), and West Africa. The criteria for grouping the
various African nations to one of the blocs· in most cases
was geographical · proximity, cultural links, and former
common colonial ties. Hence, it would be of interest to
examine whether and to what extent nations in these geographic regions (see Table X) were cohesive on the issues
under debate.

Research Design

The more specific questions which our research seeks
to answer are: What has been the primary focus of "African
po·litics" in the United Nations? What issues have the
African nations thought to be the most important confronting

Table I-A

GEOGRAPHICAL BLOCS OF AFRICAN NATIONS

CENTRAL AFRICA

Central African Republic
Congo (Brazzaville)
Burundi
Rwanda
Zaire
Sudan

EAST AFRICA

Ethiopia
Kenya
Somalia
Tanzania
Uganda
Zambia

NORTH AFRICA

Algeria
Libya
Mauritania
Morocco
Tunisia
United Arab Republic

SOUTHERN AFRICA (BLACK MAJORITY REGIMES)

Botswana
Lesotho
Malawi
Swaziland

WEST AFRICA

Cameroon
Chad
Dahomey
Equatorial Guinea
Gabon
Gambia
Ghana
Guinea
Ivory Coast
Mali
Niger
Nigeria
Republic of Cape Verde
Republic of Sao Tome & Principe

the international community and thus deserving the attention of that community in terms of resolving those issues?
Have these issues during the period under consideration
here differed from those observed in earlier periods by earlier
works? The second primary research question is: What are
the specific "political strategies" that African nations
have recommended to gain compliance to the United Nations
resolutions and principles related to the issues of concern
to them? Is the process indicative of a progressive discernible pattern over a broad array of issues? Which nations have
been the targets of African "influence" in the United Nations?

The methodology that we will use to answer these research
questions will consist primarily of content analysis of the
United Nations General Debate Speeches by African nations,
as described in Chapter II. In addition we will attempt to
provide some historical background and discussion of diplomatic and foreign policy actions by African nations, e.g. OAU
actions, which seem particularly relevent to our concerns.

Our study will be divided into five additional chapters.
The second chapter will seek to define the specific issues
which have been of most concern to African nations in the
United Nations, and on which African nations attempted to
exert "influence". This chapter will also seek to identify
the range of methods and techniques of political action or
influence African nations recommended to respond to the issues
of most concern to them in the United Nations and the international commuty. In the third, fourth, and fifth chapters
we will discuss the three issues of most concern to African
nations in the U.N. with respect to (1) identifying the
particular methods or techniques of influence favored to gain
compliance to the relevant U.N. resolutions and principles;
(2) determining the cohesiveness of African nations with
respect to the methods of influence favored (3) determining
variation along geographical lines. In chapter six, we will
discuss some general conclusions about our hypotheses and
findings.

FOOTNOTES

1. David Kay, The New Nations in the United Nations (New York, 1970), p. 1.

2. David Kay, "The Impact of African States On The United Nations," International Organization, XXIII, No. 1, Winter 1969, p. 22.

3. Sir Andrew Cohen, "The New Africa And The United Nations," in Legum, Colin, Africa: A Handbook to the Continent (New York, 1962), p. 491-499.

4. Irvine Keith, "African Nationalism And The U.N.," Current History June, 1960. Vol. 38, No. 226, p. 352-358.

5. Joan Gillespie, "Africa's Voice At The United Nations," Africa Special Report, June, 1959, Vol. 4, No. 6, P. 13-14.

6. Will Maslow, "Afro-Asian Bloc In The United Nations," Middle Eastern Affairs, November, 1957, Vol. 8, No. 11, p. 372-377.

7. Thomas Hovet, Bloc Politics In The United Nations (Cambridge 1960)

8. Vernon McKay, Africa in World Politics (Westport, Conneticut 1963)

9. Moses E. Akpan, African Goals and Diplomatic Strategies In the United Nations (North Qiuncy, Masschusetts, 1976)

10. Hovet, Africa In The United Nations, p. 22.

11. Ibid., p. 23

12. Hovet, p. 33.

13. Ibid., p. 75

14. Yassin El-Ayouty and Hugh C. Brooks, Africa And International Organization, (Netherlands, 1974).

15. Kay, New Nations un the United Nations, pg. 181

16. Robert O. Keohane, "The Study of Political Influence In The General Assembly," International Organization, Vol. 21, 1967, pp. 224.

17. Ibid., p. 224-5.

18. Ibid., p. 225.

19. Ibid.

20. Catherine Senf Manno, " Majority Decisions and Minority Responses In The U.N. General Assembly," Journal of Conflict Resolution, Vol. 10, 1966 p. 11.

21. Ibid.

22. Ibid.

23. John G. Stoessinger, The United Nations And The Super-powers (New York, 1965), p.4.

24. Stephen Goodspeed, The Nature And Function of International Organization, (New York, 1959), p. 130.

25. Ibid, p. 124.

26. Gabriella Rosner Lande, "The Effect of the Resolutions of the United Nations General Assembly", World Politics, Vol. 19, No. 1, Oct., 1966, p. 83.

27. Ibid., pp. 84-85.

28. Ibid., p. 85.

29. Ibid

30. Ibid.

31. Ibid.

32. Goodspeed, p. 116.

33. Lande, p. 84.

34. Goodspeed, p. 116.

35. Micheal Brecher, "A Framework For Research On Foreign Policy Behavior," Journal of Conflict Resolution, March, 1969, Vol. 13, No. I, p. 83.

36. Michael Brecher, "International Relations And Asian Studies: The Subordinate State System of Southern Asia," World Politics, Vol. 15, No. 2, January, 1963, p. 219.

Chapter II

Issues and Strategies

Our purpose in this chapter will be two-
fold: (1) to determine what issues were of most
concern to African nations in the United Nations
and the international community, (2) to determine the
gamut of range of strategies African nations recommended
to respond to the issues of most concern to them in the
United Nations and the international community.

An appropriate approach for our purposes is analysis
of the speeches of all African nations made in the General
debate of the Unite Nations' General Assembly. In the
General Debate sessions member nations of the United Nations
have the opportunity to formally address the assembly on the
problems confronting the international community before the
formal business of a particular session begins. The ap-
propriateness of focusing upon the U.N. General Debate is
confirmed by the observation made by the United States
Ambassador to the U.N.:

> This annual general debate serves the
> important purpose of allowing each
> member to lay before the entire Assembly,
> at the outset of our session, its major
> concerns in the international sphere.[37]

Thus, the context in which speeches are given in the General
Debate of the U.N. render them quite conducive for realizing our
purposes. Nations participate in the General Debate of the
U.N. for the purpose not only for defining the paramount issues
confronting the international community and the U.N. but also
to call for specific actions and recommendations to resolve
those problems.

The method we used to define the primary issues was
content analysis. In this chapter we provide an analysis of
all the speeches made by African nations in the General Debate
of the General Assembly for the period of 1967-1975. We could

have relied upon the memories of the personnel of the
permanent missions of each of the African nations but
decided that this would tend to rely too heavily upon the
subjectivity of individuals, who might overemphasize what
they felt personally were the most important issues. We
concluded that speech analysis would be the most objective
and reliable method for measuring the issues of concern to
African nations. By using content analysis, we were able to
identify the issues which the African nations spoke on and
determine the priorit of concern accorded to each issue.
Each and every issue discussed by an African nation in the U.N.
General debate was separately noted in the proceedings of
each session.

Issues of Concern to African Nations

The data in Graphs I-IX (Appendix I) was collected by
reading all speeches made by African nations in the General
Debate of the U.N. from 1967-1975. By examining each speech made
by each African nation for each year we were able to identify all
issues of international concern raised for each respective year.*
The percentage of African nations discussing each issue was
determined and is graphically recorded to show what specific issues
were discussed most frequently for each session. The data in
Graphs I-IX is summarized in tabular form in Table I-A. Here
the total number of speeches made by African nations for each
U.N. General Debate session between 1967-1975 is indicated in
addition to the percentage of those nations discussing issues
raised between 1967-1975 in the U.N. Debate.

As the table indicated, there were 42 different issues raised
by African nations in the U.N. Debate between 1967-1975. The
most frequently discussed issues were: Decolonization, Disarmament,
Divided Countries, Economic Development, Korea, Middle East, Sea-bed,
U.N. Organization, and Vietnam. Each of these issues was raised
by a substantial percentage of African nations during five or more
of the U.N. General Debate sessions between 1967-1975.

Table 1-A also shows the cumalative percentage of African nations
raising these issues in the U.N. over the nine sessions between
1967-1975. Table 1-B shows the percentages for the ten most
frequently raised issues. We are able to conclude from this table
that Decolonization, having been raised by 94% of all African
nations which spoke in the U.N. over the nine sessions between
1967-1975, ewas the most important issue of

-26-

*The phrase 'raised the issue' as used in this book means that
a particular issue was pointed out and discussed in General Debate
speeches as a crucial problem confronting the U.N.

ISSUES RAISED BY AFRICAN NATIONS PARTICIPATING IN THE UNITED NATIONS GENERAL DEBATE

TABLE 1-A

Issue	Percentage of African Nations Raising the Issue									
	1967	1968	1969	1970	1971	1972	1973	1974	1975	*
1. African Drought	0	0	0	0	0	0	31	25	0	6.2
2. Bangladesh	0	0	0	0	12	6	1	0	0	2.1
3. Cambodia	0	0	0	0	0	0	30	0	0	3.3
4. Chile	0	0	0	0	0	0	0	0	0	1
5. Chinese Representation	56	34	50	50	80	0	0	0	0	30
6. Cyprus	0	0	0	0	0	0	0	88	83	19
7. Czechoslovakia	0	34	0	0	0	0	0	0	0	4
8. Decolonization	96	87	93	95	88	93	100	94	97	94
9. Detente	0	0	0	0	0	0	79	22	30	14.55
10. Disarmament	56	87	63	50	52	57	48	41	56	57
11. Divided Countries	13	26	10	5	4	8	0	0	0	7
12. Economic Development	69	96	83	60	64	83	82	100	94	81
13. Energy Crisis	0	0	0	0	0	0	0	3	0	.33

Note: In the General Debate, each nation may make only one speech.

*Average %, 1967-1975

-27-

TABLE 1-A CONTINUED

Issue	Percentage of African Nations Raising the Issue									
	1967	1968	1969	1970	1971	1972	1973	1974	1975	*
14. Environment	0	0	0	5	8	27	3	0	0	4.7
15. Foreign Bases	0	0	0	0	0	3	0	0	0	.33
16. Guinea Invasion (By Portugal)	0	0	0	0	32	0	0	0	0	3.5
17. Hijacking of Aircraft	0	4	3	20	0	3	0	0	0	3.3
18. Human Rights	0	0	0	15	0	0	1	0	0	1.7
19. Hunger	0	0	0	5	0	0	6	19	0	3.3
20. Indian Ocean	0	0	0	0	0	0	0	0	27	3
21. International Cooperation	0	4	0	0	0	0	0	0	0	.44
22. International Law	0	0	3	0	0	0	6	0	0	1
23. International Relations	0	0	0	0	0	0	12	0	0	1.3
24. International Terrorism	0	0	0	0	0	32	2	0	0	3.7
25. International Women's Year	0	0	0	0	0	0	0	0	23	2.5
26. Korea	18	0	23	20	36	36	53	44	70	33.3
27. Land-Locked Countries	0	0	0	0	0	0	0	2	0	.33
28. Middle East	96	100	83	65	72	100	97	100	100	90
29. Nigeria-Biafra	13	57	60	0	0	0	0	0	0	14.4
30. Northern Ireland	0	0	0	0	0	3	0	0	0	.33

*Average %, 1967-1975.

TABLE 1-A CONTINUED

Issue	1967	1968	1969	1970	1971	1972	1973	1974	1975	*
				Percentage of African Nations Raising the Issue						
31. Outer Space Technology	9	0	0	0	0	0	0	0	0	1
32. Outlawing War	0	0	0	5	0	0	0	0	0	.55
33. Peace Keeping	0	4	0	0	0	0	0	0	0	.44
34. Population Control	0	0	0	0	0	0	0	19	0	2.7
35. Refugees	18	4	0	0	0	6	0	0	0	2.4
36. Rights of Children	0	0	0	0	0	2	0	0	0	.22
37. Sea Bed	0	4	6	30	8	21	7	50	23	17
38. South East Asia	0	0	0	0	0	0	0	0	40	4.4
39. Spanish Sahara	0	0	0	0	0	0	0	22	27	5.4
40. Uganda Asians	0	0	0	0	0	2	0	0	0	.22
41. U.N. Organization	28	0	6	30	12	26	0	3	63	19
42. Vietnam	65	60	63	45	40	76	62	0	23	48
Total number of speeches by African Nations	35	30	30	20	25	36	31	35	33	

*Average %, 1967 - 1975.

THE CUMULATIVE PERCENTAGE OF AFRICAN NATIONS IN THE UNITED NATIONS RAISING THE ISSUES THEY MOST FREQUENTLY DISCUSSED IN THE U.N. GENERAL DEBATES BETWEEN 1967-1975

TABLE 1-B

Issue	Percentage Of Nations Raising the Issue
Chinese Representation	30
Cyprus	19
Decolonization	94
Disarmament	57
Economic Development	81
Korea	33
Middle East	90
Sea-bed	17
U.N. Organization	19
Vietnam	48

concern. Second most important was the Middle East, which was raised by 90% of all African nations who spoke over the same period. The third most frequently raised issue was Economic Development, with 81% of all African nations addressing the U.N. General Debate raising the issue over the nine sessions.

The next two most frequently raised issues were Disarmament, with 57% of African nations raising the issues, and Vietnam with 48%. Other issues of substantial concern were: Korea (33%), Chinese Representation (30%), U.N. Organization (19%), and Cyprus (19%).

Strategies of Influence Used by African Nations

Using content analysis of the General Debate speeches of all African nations, we were able to identify the various strategies recommended by African nations with respect to each issue for the years between 1967-1975. We then grouped the various techniques mentioned into a number of general types of action African nations favored with respect to these issues, such as appeals, negotiations, sanctions, etc. We were then able to classify the main strategies of influence recommended by African nations in the U.N. between 1967-1975 in three major categories: (1) persuasion; (2) isolation; (3) Militant-radical confrontation. We define these categories as follows:

Persuasion

"Persusaion", as a technique influence used by African nations in the U.N. includes: a) moralistic appeals to the member nations of the U.N. and international community, b) support of diplomatic missions to appeal for the resolution of conflict, and c) support of formal negotiation efforts. When a speech calls for supports, or recommends any of these three approaches to resolving the issues of decolonization, the Middle East Crisis, or economic development, we say that the use of persuasion as a technique of influence is favored by the nation whose representative makes the speech.

Isolation

"Isolation" includes various proposals to embarrass, ostracize or cut ties with a nation to focus world attention on its violation of some 'sacred' international principle or law. This technique is manifested by recommendations of specific acts of deprivation, e.g. formal international economic sanctions, boycott and the severing of diplomatic relations. When a speech calls for or recommends these types of action as a means to force nations to comply with U.N. resolutions and principles on the issues of decolonization, the Middle East Crisis, and economic development we say that the use of isolation as a technique of influence is favored.

Militant-Radical Confrontation

The strategy of influence of militant radical confrontation involves the threat of the use or support for military action and other unprecendented actions such as expulsion of nations from the United Nations Organization to gain compliance to U.N. resolutions and principles.

While expulsion from the U.N. logically could be interpreted as a form of isolation, e.g. ostracism, we have chosen to code it in our data as a technique of militant/radical confrontation because expulsion of a nation from the organization was unprecedented in the United Nations and went beyond any action therefore taken by the international community.

When African nations in the U.N. call for such actions in their speeches before the U.N. Assembly in General Debate on the issues of decolonization, the Middle East Crisis, or economic development, we conclude that they favor gaining compliance to the U.N. principles and resolutions on these issues by using militant radical confrontation.

In coding the strategies recommended, we encountered the problem that more than one type of action might be recommended in a particular speech. In fact it was common for African nations initially to express a desire for 'persuasion" despite the fact that later in their speeches they might call for a

different strategy. In such cases, in order to determine
the appropriate coding we selected the strategy that (1)
was elaborated and discussed the most; (2) differed from
that recommended in the previous U.N. session; suggesting
a significant change in approach.

-33-

CONCLUSION

Our data and analysis of the individual speeches of African nations in the U.N. Debate reveal that while there were some 42 different issues discussed, the three most frequently discussed, and hence presumably of greatest concern, 1967-1975 were decolonization, Middle East Crisis and economic development.

Further analysis of the individual speeches of African nations on each of the three seperate issues reveal that the various strategies of influence recommended in seeking compliance to relevant U.N. resolutions and principles can be categorized as persuasion (P), isolation (I), and militant/radical confrontation (MRC). We will use these categories of influence as the basis for determining the degree of cohesion that African nations expressed in the U.N. on each issue and to express variation along geographical blocs.

FOOTNOTES

37. United Nations Document A/PV. 1562, September 21, 1967.

CHAPTER III

DECOLONIZATION: A CASE STUDY OF AFRICAN INFLUENCE
IN THE UNITED NATIONS

The purpose of this chapter will be to examine how
African nations reponded to the issue of greatest concern to
them in the U.N. between the years 1967-1975: decolonization.
This issue was seen to involve essentially the political
situation of certain African nations: South Africa, Rhodesia,
Naimbia, and the former Portugese colonies of Angola, Mozambique and Guinea Bissau. The political situation in these
states was either colonialism or white-minority rule.

We will proceed by (1) examining some relevant background
material on foreign policy actions by African nations relating
to the issue of decolonization, (2) identifying the various
strategies of influence favored by African nations to gain
compliance to the relevant U.N. resolutions and principles
on decolonization, (3) determining the percent of African
nations favoring these strategies, (4) determining variation by
geographical blocs among African nations on the issue of
decolonization.

We will first outline the U.N. resolutions and principles
that have been established by the world body on the problem of
decolonization and examine the response of African nations in
the U.N. to the issue prior to 1967, to provide historical
perspective. We will then give a more detailed explanation of
the colonial issue, or white-minority rule, in the respective
countries.

African Nations'Influence on Decolonization in the U.N., 1945-1967

In 1945 at the creation of the United Nations, as pointed
out earlier, Africa had no identity in the organization. Only
four nations from the African continent participated in the
San Francisco Conference in 1945 which created the U.N.: Egypt
South Africa, Ethiopia, and Liberia. The other African nations
were political colonies of Western Europe. It was only during
the subsequent years that most African nations were to begin
gaining independence nationhood and membership in the United
Nations had obtained membership in the United Nations.

The fifteenth session of the United Nations Assembly, in 1960, marked the point when the world organization took a positive stand against the vestiges of colonialism still existing in the world. The concern of the Assembly during this session for the issue of colonalism can be attributed to the fact that by September 1960 there was a decisively increased tempo of the disintegration of the colonial empires of Africa. The fact that seventeen former colonial territories gained admission to the U.N. at this session shaped the political context of the debate.

It was as the result of a petition of the Soviet Union that the issue of "colonialism" was placed on the agenda to be considered and discussed. "With the recommendation of the General Committee on September 28, 1960, that the Soviet item be placed on the agenda, the Assembly seemed assured of the first full scale debate in its history on the broad question of colonialism..."[38] The Soviet proposal also included a request that the standard procedure of assigning the item to an appropriate committee to be studied be by-passed, so that the issue could be considered directly in plenary session of the General Assembly. This proposal to forego standard procedure on the issue of "colonialism" won substantial support and was carried through.

The Soviet Union next offered a resolution on the issue of colonialism. Informal talks among the African and Asian nations, however. led to a decision by them to sponsor a different draft resolution on the question of colonialism. The decision was based on the belief that the Soviet draft would encounter difficulty in being passed because of its intemperate language and its demands that all leased areas and bases be removed from foreign soil. It also reflected the strong feeling that a nation which had experienced colonialism should introduce such a resolution.[39]

It was in the meetings where the actual draft resolution on colonialism was drawn up that the impact of the African influence was visible. The actual task of drafting the resolutions on colonialism among the Afro-Asian nations was relegated to a committee of six member nations consisting of three African states (Guniea, Nigeria, Senegal), and three Asian states (India, Indonesia, and Iran). The committee finally worked out a compromise draft which differed markedly from that of the Soviets.

The difference between the Afro-Asian draft resolution on colonialism and the Soviet proposal resided
basically in its time and substance. Colin Legum
summarizes the differences this way:

> This Afro-Asian draft differed from
> its Soviet counterpart in both tone and
> substance. Whereas the Soviet draft was
> both anti-colonial and anti-Western, the
> Afro-Asian draft was only anti-colonial
> and strenously avoided attacks on specific
> Western countries. ...Instead of proclaiming
> "the following demands" as in the Soviet
> draft, this draft only "declares". The
> substance of the operative paragraphs also
> differed. While the Soviet draft had de-
> manded that all colonial territories "be
> granted forthwith complete independence and
> freedom," the Afro-Asian draft spoke of
> "immediate steps" to be taken to transfer
> power, implying that the transfer could
> proceed according to an orderly timetable.
> In contrast to the Soviet draft, no mention
> is to be found in this draft of any pro-
> hibition upon foreign bases.[40]

Following the debate on the draft resolutions of the
Soviet Union and the Afro-Asian nations, the United Nations
General Assembly adopted by roll-call vote the Afro-Asian
draft which became Resolution 1514 (XV) - A "Declaration on
the Granting of Independence to Colonial Countries and Peoples."
This historic resolution called for the independence of the
remaining colonial territories. The text of the resolution
was only a declaration of principle as opposed to a demand for
the immediate and complete independence and freedom of colonial countries and peoples. The adopted resolution merely
called for steps to be taken toward the transfer of power
with no specific time limit or date for the liquidation of
colonialism to have been completed. The declaration stated:

The General Assembly,. . .

Believing that the process of liberation
is irresistible and irreversible and that,
in order to avoid serious crisis, an end
must be put to colonialism and all practices
of segregation and discrimination associated
therewith,
Welcoming the emergence in recent years
of a large number of dependent territories into
freedom and independency, and recognizing the
increasingly powerful trends towards freedom in
such territories which have not yet attained
independence,
Convinced that all peoples have an inalienable right to complete freedom, the exercise
of their sovereignty and the integrity of
their national territory,
Solemnly proclaims the necessity of bringing
to a speedy and unconditional end to colonialism
in all its forms and manifestations:
And to this end
Declares that:

1. The subjection of peoples to alien
subjegation, domination and exploitation
constitutes a denial of fundamental human
rights, is contrary to the Charter of the
United Nations and is an impediment to
the promotion of world peace and cooperation.
2. All peoples have the right to self-
determination; by virtue of that right, they
freely determine their political status and
freely pursue their economic, social and
cultural development.
3. Inadequacy of political, economic, social
or educational preparedness should never
serve as a pretext for delaying independence.
4. All armed action or repressive measures
of all kinds directed against dependent peoples
shall cease in order to enable them to exercise
peacefully and freely their right to complete
independence, and the integrity of their national territory shall be respected.

5. **Immediate steps shall be taken**, in
trust and Non-Self Governing Territories
or all other territories which have not yet
attained independence, to transfer all powers
to the peoples of those territories, without
any conditions of reservations, in accordance
with their freely expressed will and desire,
without any distinction as to race, creed or
color, in order to enable them to enjoy complete independence and freedom...[41]

After the adoption of the resolution only a few territories
were granted independence by the next U.N. session in 1961.
In fact, at this time there existed some eighty territories,
world wide, comprising a population of about seventy million
who lived under the yoke of colonialism.

In response to the lack of compliance with the Declara-
tion by member nations, the General Assembly in 1961 adopted
another resolution which reiterated and reaffirmed the 1960
Declaration. The resolution was entitled: Resolution 1654
(SVI) The Situation with Regard To The Implementation Of The
Declaration On The Granting of Independence To Colonial Countries
And Peoples. It stated:

The General Assembly,

Recalling the Declaration on the granting of
independence to colonial countries and peoples
contained in its resolution 1514 (XV) of 14
December 1960,
Bearing in mind the purpose and principles
of that Declaration,
. . .

Noting with regret that, with a few exceptions,
the provisions contained in the aforementioned
paragraph of the declaration have not been carried
out,

Noting that, contrary to the provisions of
paragraph 4 of the Declaration, armed action and
repressive measures continue to be taken in
certain areas with increasing ruthlessness
against dependent peoples, depriving them of their
perogative to exercise peacefully and freely their
right to complete independence,

. . .

-40-

Convinced that further delay in the application of the Declaration is a continuing source
of international conflict and disharmony, seriously
impedes international cooperation, and is creating
an increasingly dangerous situation in many parts
of the world which may threaten international
peace and security,

. . .

1. Solemnly reiterates and reaffirms the objectives and principles enshrined in the Declaration
on the ranting of independence to colonial countries and peoples contained in its resolution
1514 (XV) of 14 December 1960;
2. Calls upon states concerned to take action without
further delay with a view to the faithful application and implementation of the Declaration;
3. Decides to establish a Special Committee of
seventeen members to be nominated by the President
of the General Assembly at the present session;
4. Requests the Special Committee to examine the
application of the Declaration, to make suggestions
and recommendations on the progress and extent
of the implementation of the Declaration, and to
report to the General Assembly at its seventeenth
session...[42]

The resolution, while not establishing a date when all
colonial countries should be independent did create a Special
Committee as indicated comprised of Australia, Cambodia,
Ethiopia, India, Italy, Madagascar, Mali, Poland, Syria,
Tanganyika, Tunisia, Union of Soviet Socialist Republic,
United Kingdom of Great Britain and Northern Ireland, United
States of America, Uruguay, Venezuela, Yugoslavia.

Therefore, the primary U.N. principles on the issue of
decolonization were formulated by Resolution 1514 (XV) -
"A Declaration on the Granting of Independence to Colonial Countries and Peoples", and Resolution 1654 (XVI)." The situation
with regard To The Implementation of The Declaration On The
Granting Of Independence To Colonial Countries And Peoples.

It is clear from these resolutions that the United Nations
unequivocally condemned colonialism and favored the granting
of independence to said territories.

What was the U.N. response to the existence of white-
minority regimes on the African continent?

The United Nations And White-Minority Regimes

South Africa

The racial policies of the Government of South Africa
have been a concern of other independent African nations.
The official government policy of apartheid, which is the
racial separation of the majority of blacks from the minority of
whites in the social, economic and political institutions
of the society, has brought harsh criticism and objections from
other African nations. A system of unequal distribution of
power and wealth between blacks and whites, with advantages
to whites, is sanctioned and perpetuated by the policy of
apartheid. As a result, wide differences in standards of
living, formal education, health, occupation, and wages between blacks and whites exist. The whites as a result of
government policy are ensured a virtual monopoly of both power
and wealth.

The response of the U.N. to the situation in South Africa
has been threefold: (1) a constant condemnation of the racial
policies and the domination of a minority of whites over a
majority of blacks; (2) aid the victims of apartheid through
humanitarian relief programs; (3) a constant unfruitful study
of means of the U.N. to resolve the problem of South Africa.

The consideration of the racial policies of South Africa
by the United Nations began with the very first session of
the General Assembly in 1946. "The matter was then raised by
the Government of India in the form of a complaint to the
Assembly that the South African Government had enacted legislation against South Africans of Indian origin in violation of
agreements between the two Governments." [43] The broader

question of apartheid in South Africa was raised in 1952 in the U.N. Assembly under the agenda item of the "Question of Race Conflict In South Africa Resulting From The Policies of Apartheid of The Government Of The Union Of South Africa."

Between the period of 1960 when the Security Council first considered the question of apartheid, and 1967, the U.N. Assembly passed numerous resolutions on the issue of apartheid. The essence of these resolutions was a condemnation of apartheid and an appeal to South Africa to abandon the policy. As one observer noted about the resolutions on this issue:

> In the various resolutions adopted on this subject, the General Assembly and the Security Council declared that the racial policy of the Government of South Africa, and in particular its policy of apartheid, is in violation of South Africa obligations under the charter to promote the observance of human rights and fundamental freedoms for all. They repeatedly expressed in recent years their conviction that those policies had caused international friction and were seriously disturbing the maintenance of international peace and security.[44]

The U.N. actions consisted primarily of appeals to South Africa to change her policy on moral grounds as determined by the charter and to ask member states to take whatever effective actions to bring pressure on South Africa as they determined. The other actions on the problem of South Africa by the U.N. consisted of giving aid to the victims of apartheid and the establishment of various committees to study how the problem could be solved.

At the seventeenth session of the United Nations in 1962, the General Assembly requested member nations to take various diplomatic and economic measures against South Africa and created an eleven member Special Commitee on the Policies of Apartheid of the Government of the Republic of South Africa with the task of reviewing the situation and reporting to

the General Assembly and the Security Council. In
1963 and 1964 the Security Council". . . called upon
all States to cease the sale and shipment of arms and
ammunition of all types, and military vehicles to
South Africa. . ."45

With respect to the victims of apartheid the U.N.
established humanitarian programs for their assistance.
In 1964 in pursuance of a Security Council resolution the
Secretary-General created a United Nations Education and
Training Program for South Africans. The objective of
the program was to support the education and training of
South Africans abroad. This program was followed by the
creation of the United Nations Trust Fund for South Africa
in 1965 in accordance with a resolution adopted by the
General Assembly. The fund was established to provide
". . .legal assistance to persons charged under discri-
minatory and repressive legislation in South Africa; relief
for dependents of persons persecuted by the South African
Government for their opposition to the policies of apartheid
education of prisoners and their dependents; and relief for
refugees from South Africa."46

Rhodesia

Under the white minority regime of Rhodesia, some
240,000 whites rule to the exclusion of 4 million blacks.
Blacks are denied equal participation in economic and
political institutions of society through a system of racial
separation and oppression.

The Rhodesia situation of white-dominated rule was
compounded by the fact that in response to British pressure
to bring about change in its apartheid system, Rhodesia
unillaterally declared itself independent of the British
crown on November 11, 1965. The African nations refused to
recognize the new regime, and looked to Britain to correct
the situation in Rhodesia by quashing the rebellion with
force.

Britain refused to use force, insisting that sanctions
could be an effective way of solving the Rhodesian problem.
Britain through the U.N. Security Council obtained a resolution on November 20, 1965 calling on all states "to
refrain from any action that would assist the illegal
regime, and, in particular, to desist from providing arms,
equipment, and military material, and to do their utmost
in order to break all economic relations..."including an em-
bargo on oil and petroleum products."[47] The British aim was
to disrupt the Rhodesian economy to bring progress toward
universal suffrage. The resolution passed by the U.N.
Security Council instituted voluntary economic sanctions
against Rhodesia.

Britain felt compelled to offer some further proposal
when the OAU, on December 3, 1965, resolved to break off all
relations with Britain if the Rhodesian Government was not
crushed. Prime Minister Wilson responded by pledging to the
African nations that Britain would push for mandatory economic
sanctions if the Rhodesian regime had not been suppressed by
December of 1966.[48]

A year of voluntary sanctions did not force Rhodesia
to capitulate to the British goals. The Smith regime remained
intransigent. When the voluntary sanctions failed, Britain
asked the Security Council to impose mandatory economic
sanctions against Rhodesia after talks between Prime Minister
Wilson of the U.K. and Prime Minister Smith of Rhodesia broke
down in 1966. Manadatory sanctions were imposed by the Security
Council on December 16, 1966 when:

> . . . The United Nations Security Council
> decided to forbid United Nations member states
> to purchase certain commodities from Rhodesia.
> These banned commodities constituted Rhodesia's
> most important exports. In addition to this ban,
> the Security Council ordered that no member
> nations were to export oil, ammunition aircraft
> or motor vehicles to Rhodesia.[49]

This resolution represented the first time that the United
Nations had imposed mandatory, collective, economic sanctions.
Although the sanctions did not bring Rhodesia to accept
majority rule their historic significance remained.

Mozambique, Angola, Guinea Bissau, Cape Verde, Sao Tome
and Principe

Portugal was more recalcitrant than Britain and France
in granting independence to her colonial possessions in
Africa. These territories did not obtain independence until after 1973, while the other European colonial territories were granted independence during the early 1960's.
The former Portuguese colonies thus constituted a major
part of the problem of decolonization for most of the
period covered by this study.

Namibia (South-West Africa)*

Namibia was a mandate territory handed over for administration to South Africa after World War I under the
League of Nations' Mandate System. The former German
colony has come to be ruled under the racial laws of
apartheid as applied in South Africa, to the point that
it has become a mini-South Africa.

The U.N. General Assembly on October 27, 1966 approved
a resolution which recognized the inalienable right of
Namibians to freedom and independence, terminated South
Africa's mandate over the territory and established a 14-
member states' committee with the assigned task of recommending practical steps by which Namibia should be administered.

This committee met with failure due to the fact that it
could not find agreement among its own members on how to
implement the Assembly's decision terminating South Africa's
mandate. The U.N. General Assembly responded with more
decisive action in Resolution 2145 (XXI) in which it set
June,1968 as a date for the achievement of independence for
Namibia. In addition,the resolution provided for the transfer
of the mandate, for the U.N. to enter Namibia to take over the
administration and for consultation with Namibians to achieve
their independence. The outcome of this resolution was

---

*Southwest Africa is commonly referred to by proponents of
independence as Namibia, its native name, which we will use
generally in this study.

described by Legum:

> So, the U.N. found itself committed in 1968
> to the charade of setting up a U.N. Council
> for South West Africa, with Administrators
> to take over control from the South African
> Administration. This council was supposed to
> enter the mandated territory on April 5.
> They got as far as Zambia but, unable to get
> a plane willing to take the risk of flying
> them into the territory, they tamely returned
> to base at New York with the South Africans
> rejoicing over the ease with which they had
> seen off 'the paper tiger'.[50]

In a later move by the U.N. Security Council, it considered the problem of Namibia, sought an advisory opinion in 1967 from the World Court on the specific question: "What are the legal consequences for States of the continued presence of South Africa in Namibia, notwithstanding S.C. resolution 276 (1970)?"[51] This time the court's decision state categorically in 1971 that South African presence in the territory of South West Africa was illegal.

In spite of the U.N. General Assembly's resolutions terminating its mandate over Namibia and the World Court's ruling on the illegality of its presence in Namibia, South Africa has maintained its control over the territory.

African Influence on Decolonization In The U.N.: 1967-1975

The problem of the former Portugese colonial territories of Angola, Mozambique, Cape Verde, Guinea Bissau, Sao Tome & Principe and the white minority regimes of Rhodesia, South Africa and Namibia, was perceived by African nations as the problem of "southern Africa"; which became the main focus of "decolonization" as the issue of paramount concern to African nations in the United Nations in the period 1967-1975.

It was obvious in 1967 that U.N. involvement and action in the problem of white dominated regimes in southern Africa had not resulted in resolving or improving the situation there.

Despite its various actions with regard to Rhodesia,
Namibia, South Africa, and the former Portugese colonies
of Mozambique, Angola, and Guinea Bissau, the problem of decolonization remained unchanged by the end of the 1960's.
Although the U.N. had passed resolutions calling for the
end of colonialism, had applied economic sanctions, and
had obtained relevant judicial decisions from the World
Court, the political condition of black Africans in southern
Africa had not improved.

Thus, it was very clear by 1967 that the hope of the
African nations in the U.N. that their participation in the
world body could bring about a rapid change in the situation
in southern Africa was proved false. 1967 was to mark a new
phase in the manner in which these nations would seek to
exert influence in the U.N. on the issue of southern Africa
This new phase was, perhaps, embarked upon by African nations,
because their number in the U.N. was increasingly significant.

The various techniques of influence favored by African
nations in obtaining compliance to resolutions on decolonization
between 1967-1975 can be grouped in the following categories:
Persuasion, Isolation and Militant/Radical Confrontation.
These categories were derived from an analysis of the speeches
by African nations in the U.N. General Debates. The main points
of this analysis are detailed in Appendix II. The data used
throughout this chapter to answer our research questions will
be based on the information contained in Appendix II. The
appendix lists all African nations who were members of the
U.N. for each respective year; indicates whether they made a
speech in debate; whether they discussed the issue of decolonization in their speech, their broad policy position on
the issue, and the techniques of influence recommended. The
data on the issue of decolonization are summarized in Tables
II, III, IV, and V, and discussed below.

Persuasion

The data in Table II show the main techniques of influence
that were favored by African nations in the U.N. on the issue
of decolonization between 1967-1975. The table indicates the
various actions explicitly recommended. If a nation for any

48

INFLUENCE TECHNIQUES FAVORED BY AFRICAN NATIONS IN THE UNITED NATIONS ON THE ISSUE OF DECOLONIZATION

TABLE - II

	'67	'68	'69	'70	'71	'72	'73	'74	'75
Algeria	NR	NS	NR	MRC	NR	P	I	NR	NR
Botswana	NR	P	P	NS	NS	NS	NS	P	NS
Burundi	I	P	P	NS	NS	MRC	MRC	MRC	NS
Cameroon	NR	P	NS	ND	P	MRC	NS	MRC	MRC
Central African Republic	NS	NS	MRC	NS	P	P	NR	MRC	NS
Chad	NR	P	P	NS	NR	NR	NS	P	NR
Congo (Brazzaville)	NR	NS	NR	MRC	NR	MRC	P	P	MRC
Dahomey	NS	NS	NS	NS	NR	P	P	MRC	NR
Democratic Republic of Sao Tome & Principe	-	-	-	-	-	-	-	-	NS
Ethiopia	NR	I	P	NS	P	I	MRC	MRC	NS
Equatorial Guinea	NS	NS	NS	NS	NS	ND	MRC	MRC	
Gabon	P	NR	NR	NS	NR	P	NR	NR	NR
Gambia	I	I	NS	MRC	NS	P	NS	P	NS
Ghana	MRC	I	NS	P	P	MRC	MRC	P	I

Key -- I=Isolation -=Non-Member of U.N. ND=No Discussion of this issue NR=No Recommendation
NS=No Speech P=Persuasion MRC=Militant Radical Confrontation on this issue.

49

TABLE-II CONTINUED

	'67	'68	'69	'70	'71	'72	'73	'74	'75
Guinea	NS	P	MRC	P	MRC	MRC	MRC	NR	NS
Ivory Coast	NS	NS	P	NS	P	P	NS	P	NS
Kenya	P	P	I	I	P	I	MRC	I	MRC
Lesotho	P	P	NS	NS	NS	NS	MRC	MRC	NR
Liberia	P	P	NS	NR	NR	MRC	MRC	MRC	P
Libya	NR	I	NR	MRC	MRC	MRC	MRC	MRC	NR
Madagascar	NR	P	NR	ND	P	NR	NR	NS	NR
Malawi	P	ND	NS	NS	NS	P	NS	NS	NS
Mali	NR	NS	P	NS	I	MRC	I	NR	NR
Mauritania	P	NR	P	NS	NR	NR	NR	NR	I
Morocco	P	P	NR	MRC	MRC	MRC	NR	NR	NR
Niger	ND	NS	NS	NS	P	I	P	P	NS
Nigeria	P	NR	MRC	NS	NR	MRC	MRC	NR	MRC
Peoples' Republic of Mozambique	-	-	-	-	-	-	-	-	MRC

TABLE – II CONTINUED

	'67	'68	'69	'70	'71	'72	'73	'74	'75
Republic of Cape Verde	–	–	–	–	–	–	–	–	NS
Rwanda	P	P	N	P	NR	P	NR	ND	MRC
Senegal	ND	NR	P	NS	NR	I	MRC	NR	MRC
Sierra Leone	P	P	MRC	MRC	I	I	I	I	I
Somalia	P	I	NR	NR	NR	MRC	MRC	NS	MRC
Sudan	P	P	NR	I	P	NR	NR	NS	NR
Swaziland	–	NS	NR	NS	NS	NS	NS	P	NS
Togo	I	P	NS	I	I	MRC	NS	NR	P
Tunisia	P	I	NR	MRC	NR	P	ND	ND	P
Uganda	I	P	NR	NS	P	ND	NS	MRC	MRC
United Arab Republic	ND	ND	NS	I	I	ND	ND	MRC	MRC
United Republic of Tanzania	P	P	MRC	MS	MRC	MRC	MRC	MRC	MRC
Upper Volta	NR	NS	I	NS	MRC	MRC	P	NR	NR
Zaire	I	P	P	NS	NS	P	MRC	P	NR
Zambia	P	P	I	I	MRC	MRC	MRC	P	MRC

51

particular year did not speak in the U.N. debate at all,
or on the issue of decolonization in particular, this is
so indicated. A third possibility is indicated as well:
if a nation made a speech in debate and raised the issue
of decolonization, but refrained from recommending any
specific course of action for bringing about decolonization.
Hence the data show the particular position taken by every
African nation on the issue of decolonization in the U.N.
Debate between 1967 and 1975.

The various techniques of influence favored have been
grouped under the three categories: persuasion (P), isolation
(I), and militant/radical confrontation (MRC). Table III
summarizes the data on the issue of decolonization in
percentages. The percentages of African nations recommending
the various techniques of influence on this issue, as well
as the percentage making no recommendation, are indicated for
each year from 1967-1975.

Table III shows that "Persuasion" as a technique of
influence constituted the plurality position of African nations
in the U.N. on the issue of decolonization between 1967 and
1971. Our data does not show that the majority of African
nations in the United Nations favored the use of persuasion
techniques since on the average in those years nearly 49%
of the African nations did not make any recommendations for
action on the issue.

Despite this high percentage of silence by African
nations on the issue of decolonization, those nations which
did make recommendations of action favored persuasion between
1967-1971. The cumulative average of African nations calling
for persuasion as the technique for resolving the issue of
decolonization between 1967-1971 is 27%. This constituted the
plurality of African nations which spoke in the U.N. debate
on the issue of decolonization between 1967-1971.

In their addresses, African nations condemned states for
not adhering to the resolutions of the U.N. body pertaining
to colonialism and white-minority rule. Then they made an
appeal based on moral principles which the United Nations

PERCENTAGE BREAKDOWN OF VARIOUS ACTIONS RECOMMENDED BY AFRICAN NATIONS ON THE ISSUE OF DECOLONIZATION IN THE UNITED NATIONS

TABLE-III

		1967	1968	1969	1970	1971	1972	1973	1974	1975
PERSUASION	Negotiation	10	10	10	8	12	15	2	5	7
	Appeal	29	31	10	0	13	11	8	20	0
	Total	39	41	20	8	25	26	10	25	7
ISOLATION		5	15	13	10	10	13	8	2	7
MILITANT/RADICAL CONFRONTATION	Support Armed Struggle	1	0	3	18	10	3	27	5	20
	Expulsion From United Nations	0	0	2	0	5	31	8	23	8
	Total	1	0	5	18	15	34	35	28	28
NO ACTION RECOMMENDED		54	44	55	65	50	27	48	43	58

Percentages do not always total 100 because of rounding off

53

represented: self-determination, justice for all, equal
rights of nations. The speech made by Liberia during the
twenty-second U.N. General Debate session in 1967 typifies
the many speeches of African nations during this period:

> ...The inherent right to self-determination
> cannot be denied, and the repressive measures
> by Portugal, with all the assistance of
> its NATO allies, cannot kill this right. . .
>
> The United Nations should not sit idly by while
> Portugal flouts its decisions and recommendation,
> disregards its principles and violates the obli-
> gations of the Charter. Such insults and af-
> fronts are bound to have an adverse effect on
> the prestige of the Organization. . . . .
>
> Thus, sanctions are being contemptibly violated
> by some countries and the United Kingdom seems to
> be involved in this indirectly. . . .
>
> After virtually encouraging the Smith regime to
> rebel with an assurance that the United Kingdom
> would not intervene militarily, if it did, we
> are witnessing actions and motions supposedly
> designed to bring down the regime without the
> use of force, actions that are apparently half-
> hearted and known to be ineffective. This is
> indeed a very serious matter. The rights and
> interests of 4 million Africans are being sac-
> rifices on the altar of expendiency while in-
> effectual acts designed to hoodwink us are pro-
> posed and efficient acts are feebly executed.
> . . .and the pathetic and lamentable, visible
> effect is that the United Nations has been made
> to appear impotent and powerless to make its
> actions effective. Even inaction would not
> have been as deplorable as the present situation
> is . . . .[52]

In 1969, the commitment of African nations to peaceful
persuasion as a means for resolving the problem of southern
Africa was made explicit in the Lusake Manifesto, a joint
statement agreed to by representative of East and Central

African states meeting in April 1969 in Lusake, Zambia.
The fact that the Lusaka Manifesto on Southern Africa was
a commitment to moral persuasion, negotiation, and diplomacy as a means of peaceful settlement of the problem of
colonialism.is evident in its text;

> On the objective of liberation as thus
> defined, we can neither surrender nor
> compromise. We have always preferred
> and we still prefer, to achieve it with-
> out physical violence. We would prefer to
> negótiate rather than destroy, to talk rather
> than kill. We do not advocate violence,
> we advocate an end to the violence against
> human dignity which is not being perpetrated
> by the oppressors of Africa. . .[53]

Although the Manifesto was drawn up by the thirteen
African states of East and Central Africa,it was approved
by the Organization of African Unity and thus represented
the viewpoint of the African nations in the United Nations.
Moreover, African nations formally presented the Manifesto
to the United Nations body and asked that it associate itself with the document.

The Manifesto was formally presented by the President
of the Federal Republic of Cameroon at the twenty-fourth
session of the United Nations in 1969. On this occassion
the Manifesto became an international proclamation that
African nations were committed to persuasive and peaceful
methods of resolving the problem of southern Africa.

At the same time the Manifesto became an instrument of
the persuasive techniques of influence because on the very
occasion President Ahidjo appealed to the the nations to take
action to correct the situation in southern Africa. During
the twenty-fourth session of the U.N. President Ahidjo said:

> 1. I am present here today in quite a different
> capacity: I have been chosen by the Assembly
> of Heads of State and Government of the

55

Organization of African United to present to the
General Assembly of the United Nations a manifesto
on Southern Africa and it is on behalf of all peoples
of Africa, concerned with the fate of their continent
as with that of all mankind, that I have the privilege
and honour of addressing you today...

It is nine years now since the adoption of the
United Nations Declaration on the Granting of Independence to Colonial Countries and Peoples
(Resolution 1514 XV). We are justified in beginning
to question whether there us a genuine desire on the
part of the international community to work effectively
for the success of the struggle of the peoples of
Africa, and particularly those of the sourthern part
of our continent, to achieve their lawful rights to
freedom and independence.

In Namibia and in the territories under Portugese
rule, in Zimbabwe and in South Africa, we see the
same insolent scorn for pertinent resolutions
of the United Nations. It i now evident that this
defiant attitude to world opinion would not be
possible without the support of certain powerful
international interests and, indeed, of some Governments, which are thus betraying their obligation
towards mankind and the international community.

It is also clear that this attitude constitutes a
decided threat to international peace and security
Through its Manifesto in Southern Africa, the Organization of African Unity once again solemnly appeals to
international opinion, the pressure of which can, it
believes, play a decisive role. . . .[54]

That the Marifesto symbolized the commitment of African nations
to peaceful and persuasive methods is further seen in the manner
in which African nations perceived the document. The

56

Cameroon delegate observed in 1970 in reference to the Manifesto that : "Africa spoke with one voice when my colleague, His Excellency El Hadj Ahmadou Ahidjo, President of the Republic of Cameroon presented the Lusaka Manifesto to the 24th session of the General Assembly."[55] Zambia, one of the most active African nations involved in the issue of southern Africa summarized the political significance of the Manifesto when it observed at the next session of the U.N. Assembly:

> It is vital for all of us to recognize that the Manifesto provides us with our last slim chance of preventing a racial holocaust in southern Africa. Moreover, whether this opportunity is seized will depend more on the West than on Africa. The African states have done their part in extending the hand of friendship. It is up to the West now to grasp it eagerly and energetically.[56]

Thus it is clear that African nations interpreted the Manifesto as an attempt to persuade other nations in the U.N. to take peaceful actions to bring about political change in southern Africa. The Lusaka Manifesto was an outward expression in 1969 that African nations were desirous of and amenable to the use of peaceful means of settling the problem of southern Africa.

African nations, committed to this strategy of solving the problem of decolonization, acted upon this commitment by engaging also in dialogue and diplomatic talks with nations about southern Africa to persuade them to take effective actions to contribute to the solution of the situation. African nations directed these talks primarily to the superpowers assuming that these nations were in the best position to exert actions that could be effective in solving the problem of southern Africa. The primary target of talks was the United States.

In 1970, the Secretary of State of the United States was received and engaged in diplomatic talks in ten African nations, Morocco, Tunisia, Ethiopia, Kenya, Zambia, Congo, Cameroon, Nigeria, Ghana, and Liberia. It was the first diplomatic tour by an American Secretary of State to Africa. This was a

significant trip in terms of its possible outcome for
the development of a new American foreign policy toward
Africa. The Secretary of State, William P. Rogers stated
that his purpose was "to ask African leaders what the
United States could do that would be most helpful to
them...in terms of partnership and friendship."[57] The
anticipated focus of the talks with African leaders which
the U.S. Secretary of State would engage in on his tour
was no mystery to the observers of international affairs.
One news account succinctly noted the significance of
Secretary Rogers' tour to Africa:

> Mr.Rogers faces several delicate problems in
> translating the goodwill intended in making
> the trip into politics that will satisfy the
> hopes of African political leaders.
> One of these problems is that of the white-
> minority governments of southern Africa under
> which the large black majorities of Rhodesia,
> South Africa, South-West Africa, and the Portu-
> geses territories of Angola and Mozambique have
> been denied full political rights.
> Most African leaders hope that the United
> States will take a stronger position of con-
> demnation against the white governments and
> specifically, that the State department will
> close the American consulate in Rhodesia....[58]

The nature of the talks that African leaders held with Secretary
Rogers is perhaps represented by those held between the
Secretary and the President of Zambia, Kenneth Kaunda.   On
February 17, 1970 President Kaunda held three-hours of talks
with the U.S. Secretary of State.   "Specifically, Mr. Kaunda
asked Mr. Rogers to use the influence of the United States
to get Portugal to respond positively to the so-called
Lusaka Manifesto issued by Central and East African nations
in April, 1969."[59] Mr. Kaunda on this occasion represented
the sentiments of some African leaders when "..he told
Mr. Rogers that the United States was "about the only power..
that could help solve the racial problems of southern Africa
and that he wanted to see involvement of the U.S.

in the solution of this problem."[60]   Mr. Kaunda's appeal
to the United States was based on this specific argument
to Secretary Rogers:

> ...the United States should concentrate its
> efforts on trying to influence Portugul to
> make at least some long-range commitment to
> self-rule by Black Africans.
> The United States is "in a very special
> postition to influence the course of events,"
> he said. The United States could influence
> Portugal, its ally in the North Atlantic Treaty
> Organization, to grant independence to her
> African territories and heavy American in-
> vestment in South Africa gives the United
> States influence there for political reform,
> he added.[61]

Secretary Rogers conferred with the Secretary General
of the Organization of African Unity, Diallo Telli of Guniea
while on his tour of African nations in 1970. On behalf of
African nations Secretary Telli told Secretary Rogers "that
the United States should show the same energy' in opposing
suppression of Blacks in southern Africa by minority governments as it had sown in fighting fascism in World War II."[62]

The diplomatic talks between African leaders and the
United States were to continue in 1971. The Vice President of
the United States held talks with the Emperor of Ethiopia,
Haile Selassie on July 10, 1971. Vice President Spiro Agnew
held formal discussion with the Emperor for 40 minutes in
the capital of Ethiopia. Although the topics of discussion
were not disclosed the nature of the talks were well implied
by the remarks made by Haile Selassie in a toast to the
Vice President on this occasion. As a correspondent observed
the occasion he reported:

> The Emperor in a toast to the Vice President,
> cited "the friendly and long-standing relations
> between the two countries," and spoke briefly
> about a matter long close to his heart--African
> unity.
> In an appartent reference to the white
> supremacist policies of Rhodesia and South Africa
> the Emperor spoke of the "struggle" for the total
> liberation of Africa, the accelerated development
> and the attainment of durable peace.
> "We are confident," he went on, " that Africa
> in her present dedicated endeavors will have the

continued support of the peace-loving
peoples of the United States in the
attainment of these noble goals."[63]

The Vice President of the United States visited Kenya and
the Congo following his conference with the Emperor of
Ethipia.

The Chief of State of Mauritania, President Moktar
Ould Dahdah, addressed the United Nations Assembly on be-
half of the Organization of Unity and conferred with the
President of the United States in the fall of 1971. President
Dahdah presented Africa's case against colonialism before the
United Nations as chairman of the Organization of African
Unity. On the issue of southern Africa in his address before
the U.N., President Dahdah noted "...that aid by NATO to
Portugal...was responsible for the long colonial war in
Mozambique, Angola, and Portugese Guinea."[64] He further
condemned and indicted the "great powers" for prolonging the
problem of southern Africa by supporting the white minority
governments of South Africa and Rhodesia.

The Chief of State conferred with President Richard Nixon
for 40 minutes on Spetember 30, 1971 at the White House.
Even though the specifics of the talks were not disclosed
Mr. Dahdah was in the United States at the same time to present
the case of the OAU on colonialism before the United Nations
Assembly.

United States policy toward southern Africa was made
clear in 1971 by Richard Nixon in policy proclamations. The
essence of the Nixon policy toward Africa was that while it
gave lip service in opposition to systems based on racial
discrimination it spelled out no definite action. In fact
Nixon made it clear that the United States did not want involvement in African controversies. All the United States
desired in terms of Africa was that it not be plunged in
major power conflicts or cold war politics. It was about this
same time that Britain decided to resume the sale of arms to
South Africa.

A note of caution perhaps is necessary to prevent oversimplifying the implications of our data in general and particularly with respect here to the use of persuasion as a technique of influence by African nations on the issue of decolonization. It is by no means to be inferred from our data that the use of persuasion had temporal bounds. African nations tended to employ persuasuin techniques after 1971 under two primary conditions: (1) when leadership in the superpower nations changed; (2) when the white-minority regimes themselves made definite overtures for negotiation of the issue to African nations. However, African nations specifically stipulated conditions which had to be met by the white-minority regimes if they were to engage in negotiation on the issue of decolonization in 1975. This was done in light of the declaration by African nations in 1971 of a "rejection of dialogue" as a means of resolving the issue. For at the eighth annual meeting of the Organization of African states in June 1971 in Addis Ababa, the majority of black African unity approved a resolution forbidding any independent black states from engaging in diplomatic dialogue with the white government of South Africa. The declaration said "...that no African state should make an approach to the South African Government without the Organization's approval and unless South Africa first begin discussions with her own population."[65]

This resolution was the culmination of a debate between some African states, mainly West African, who wanted to accept the overtures of South Africa to join her in dialogue over the issue of southern Africa in 1971. The Ivory Coast President, Houphouet-Boigny, had urged black African countries to respond to South Africa's overtures without reservations because apartheid was "...a matter within the domestic jurisdiction of South Africa and it is not by force that it will be eradicated."[66] However, before passing the resolution rejecting dialogue at the 1971 OAU meeting most African nations expressed the belief that to engage in talks with South Africa before some reform in racial policy by that Government would block efforts to isolate it internationally. Yet, whether the resolution was going to prevent African nations such as the Ivory Coast, Malawi, and others who voted against it from engaging in dialogue with South Africa was not then known. And as time

unfolded several African nations specifically, the
Ivory Coast, Liberia, and Malawi did engage in talks
with the Prime Minister of South Africa on the problem
of southern Africa.

President Kenneth Kaunda visited the new President of
the United States, Gerald Ford, in April 1975 and asked that
the U.S. take a new stance toward Africa in its foreign policy,
making reference specifically to the problem of southern
Africa. And the Foreign Secretary of Britain, James Callaghan,
conferred with President Julius K. Nyerere of Tanzania on
January 7, 1975 when he was winding up his consultations with
African leaders over a search for a Rhodesian settlement.
Although the details of these talks were not disclosed it was
confirmed that they focused on the situation in southern Africa.

Isolation

The data in Table III shows with respect to the technique of isolation that it did not have significant support by
African nations even apart from the high percentage of nations
that remained silent in debate as already alluded to earlier.
In no single year between 1967-1975 in the U.N. did over 15%
of all the African nations recommend the use of isolation as a
technique for influencing the issue of decolonization. The
cumulative average of support for isolation by African nations
between the years from 1967-1975 in the U.N. Debate was 9% of
all African nations.

Therefore, our data does not confirm isolation as a
distinct stage of influence on the issue of decolonization.
Table II does not reveal any period between 1967-1975 in the
U.N. when the use of isolation maintained even a plurality of
support among African nations in their recommendations on the
issue of decolonization.

It is likely that the main reason why African nations were
not vociferous in the General Debate speeches in favor of
techniques of isolation resides in the facts that (1) the
United Nations had failed to be successful in employing the
technique against South Africa and Rhodesia in the application
of economic sanctions; (2) African nations themselves had
used Isolation without success prior to 1967 in their bilateral
relations with South Africa; (3) efforts to use techniques

of isolation in the period 1967-1975 also seemed unsuccessful in securing significant change in southern Africa; (4) the inevitable spill-over effects African nations themselves would suffer in their economic relationships with nations from which they withdrew diplomatic recognition restrained their free application of this technique

African nations had directed this technique mainly at the white-minoryt regimes of South Africa and Rhodesia. As early as 1963 when the Organization of African union was founded, African nations agreed to isolate the white southern African regimes by severing certain bilateral relations with those states. They did this by (1) breaking off diplomatic and consular relations between all African states and the governments of Portugal and South Africa; (2) forbidding the import of goods from these two countries; (3) closing African ports and airports to the ships and planes from these two countries; (4) forbidding the planes of these two countries to fly over the territories of the independent black African states.

African nations did not actively seek isolation and ostracization of white-minority regime nations in the United Nations until 1972. It was in this year that they began to seize every opportunity that presented itself to force a confrontation with the white-minority regimes. One area that has presented highly visible opportunities for this tactic of influence has been international sports events.

In 1968 African nations through the Supreme Council for Sports in Africa, which was organized in 1966, protested and threatened a boycott of the 1978 Olympic games because of the readmission of South Africa to the Olympics for that year. Originally, South Africa had been barred from the 1964 Olympics in Japan by a decision of the Internation Olympic Committee (I.O.C.) due exclusively to its apartheid policy in sports. This decision by the I.O.C. came about as a result of applying the general standards and rules with respect to choosing participants in the games. The source and nature of the 1964

63

decisions to exclude South Africa from the Olympics of
that year were succinctly traced in the following New
York Times news account:

> The International Olympic Committee
> tonight withdrew its invitation to
> South Africa to compete in the 1964
> Summer Olympic Games in Tokyo because
> of its policy of racial segregation
> in sports. . . South Africa, Brundage
> said President of I.O.C., " has accom-
> plished many things" toward meeting I.O.C.
> requirements but still has not fulfilled
> all the Olympic rules.
> He said firmly that South Africa still
> was a recognized member of the I.O.C. and
> that withdrawal of the invitation to the
> Tokyo games does not mean loss of member-
> ship.
> He said that the South African committee
> all white- has been able to give a guarantee
> that selection trials for that country's
> Tokyo team will be made outside the nation
> if necessary to allow non-whites to compete
> with whites.
> Brundage said the IOC also welcomed the
> South African news that the Johannesburg
> Government has agreed to make no trouble over
> giving non-white athletes proper passports for
> Tokyo.
> Brundage said, however, that the South African
> Committee failed to meet the third test set by
> I.O.C. that requires the South African Committee
> to meet I.O.C. standards by clearly and publicily
> opposing racial segregation in sports- both in
> games playing and in sports administration."[67]

Unlike the 1968 threatened boycott, a similar episode
in 1972 was directly motivated by opposition to the apartheid
system of Rhodesia. The National Olympic Committee of Africa
announced that 32 African nations would withdraw from the
1972 World Olympics held in Munich West Germany if the

International Olympic Committee recognized the
credentials of the Rhodesian athletes.

The dispute centered around the International
Olympic Committee's decision, a year before, that in order
for Rhodesia's athletes to participate in the games they
must participate as British subjects, using the British
flag and national anthem, the old British colony name of
"Southern Rhodesia", and British passports. The 43 member
Rhodesian team did not possess British passports.

The matter was considered by the International Olympic
Committee's Executive Board after a threatened walk-out
by African nations and West German Chancellor Willy Brandt's
appeal to resolve the dispute in order to prevent damaging
West German relations with Black Africa. The international
Olympic Committee met for four days to consider the matter.
A nine-member African delegation appeared before the committee
and insisted that the African bloc would quit the games if
Rhodesia was not ousted. The International Olympic Committee
finally voted to bar Rhodesia from participating in the 20th
Olympic Games.

About 1973 black African nations demanded that Rhodesia
be excluded from the 1976 Olympic games. Following an investigation in 1974 of formal charges made against Rhodesia by
black African nations, the International Olympic Committee was
prepared to make a decision. "The International Olympic Committe
under pressure from black African Countries, voted to withdraw
its recognition of Rhodesia and exclude it from the 1976 Olympic
Games."68 The purpose behind requesting that Rhodesia be
barred from participating in the 1976 games is clear in the re-
action of African nations to the committee's decision. One
observer commented on that response when he said:

> The Supreme Council for Sport in Africa, which
> said it represents 43 Black and North African
> countries, hailed today's vote by the I.O.C.
> at its annual meeting, "This is a victory for
> the world," said Abraham Ordia, a Nigerian who
> heads the Council. He termed the vote a rejection
> of the "pernicious philosophy of apartheid". . .69

65

Thus isolation has historically been selectively used by African nations against the white-minority regimes themselves. Although actually used by African nations, techniques of "Isolation" do not constitute a stage in their attempts to exert influence within the U.N., but such techniques were cautiously used, lacking cohesive support, in the period 1967 to 1975.

Militant/Radical Confrontation

A major shift in strategy by African nations on the issue of decolonization occured in 1972, as indicated by the data in Table III. The table shows that between 1972 and 1975 African nations in the U.N. favored means of militant/radical confrontation to influence the process of decolonization. Again, the largest number of African nations refrained from either speaking at all in debate or recommending a course of action. Nevertheless, a majority of those African nations which spoke favored the use of militant/radical confrontaion. The cumulative percentage of African nations which recommended no action, including those making no speech, on the issue of decolonization was 44% of all Afican nations in the U.N. for the period between 1972-1975. The cumulative percentage of those who spoke and made recommendations who favored militant/radical confrontation was 31% of all African nations. The remaining African nations who spoke favored the use of techniques of persuasion (17%, 1972-1975) or isolation (8%, 1972-1975).

It is clear that the plurality of support between 1972-1975 as expressed in the U.N. Debate by African nations was for militant/radical confrontation techniques of influence on the issue of decolonization.

The address of Ethiopia at the twenty-eight session of the U.N. Assembly typifies this change in tone of a growing number of African nations:

....We believe that the United Nations
has a responsibility to assist those who,
by fighting for their rights to self-determination and independence, are also
fighting for the respect of the principles
that are embodied in the Charter of the
United Nations. The recognition by the U.N.

66

of the legitimacy of the struggle of
colonial peoples must be completed with
the resolve to render not only moral but
also material assistance to the liberation
struggle.[70]

In 1972 at the ninth session of the Organization of
African Unity meeting at Rabat, Morocco, African nations
began to clearly and categorically reject dialogue or
persuasion as a means of solving the issue of decolonization.
The tone of this meeting of African nations which has been
described "as the spirit of Rabat" was highly militant.
This tone was demonstrated by an unequivocal rejection of
"dialogue" between African nations and South Africa as a
practical means of resolving the issue of decolonization of
southern Africa. This tone resulted in the adoption of
certain policies by the O.A.U. nations. Zdenek Cervenka
summarized the important policy decisions adopted:

1. The Assemly of Heads of State and
   Government unanimously decided to
   increase by 50 percent contributions
   to the Special Fund administered by
   the Liberation committee. King Hassan
   II of Morocco pledged a contribution
   of one million dollars.

2. For the first time, the representatives
   of Africa's thirteen liberation movements were allowed to speak at the
   meeting of the Council of Ministers on
   matters concerning the liberation struggle, and to attend the closed session
   of the Assembly.

3. The membership of the Liberation Committee
   was enlarged from 13 to 17 members
   (the new members being Cameroon, Congo,
   Ghana, Libya, Mauritania, and Morocco).

4. The O.A.U.'s Defense Commission was asked to prepare a detailed military plan of regional defense to ensure that if any country is attacked, it will be able to rely on immediate military support from its neighbors.

5. In the recommendation of special measures to be adopted on decolonization and the struggle against apartheid and racial discrimination, O.A.U. members were asked to provide transit facilities for all arms and war material destined to the African liberation movements.

6. Member states of the O.A.U. were asked to make available both arms and men, and to place them at the disposal of the proposed Executive Secretariat of Defense. They would be employed in counter-acting Portugese aggression.[71]

Before 1972 African nations' opinion was that national liberation movements in southern Africa should shoulder the full responsibility of their guerrilla wars with only the support of independent African states e.g. material and technical; now "the consensus at Rabat was to involve armies of African independent states directly in the armed struggle in order to liquidate Portugese colonialism..."[72]
By 1973 the consensus of African nations was that the problem of southern Africa could only be solved by escalated military efforts. Thus, several African states actually expanded their military role in the military efforts of the liberation movements of Angola, Mozambique, Rhodesia, and South Africa. This commitment to escalated military involvement to resolve the problem of southern Africa was further evidenced at the Oslo Conference of African nations held in 1973 from April 9-14 in Oslo, Norway.

The Oslo Conference restricted itself to the problem of southern Africa. It was attended by representatives of all the liberation movements of southern Africa, U.N. experts

who had been involved in the issue of decolonization, and
non-governmental organizations and agencies which had involved themselves in this issue. The conference was to
provide for the presentation of ideas and views with the
aim of arriving at practical methods of effecting change
in the situation in southern Africa. The conference was
organized into two committees of the whole with cor-
responding agendas:

> Committee I was to consider moral and material
> assistance to the peoples of South Africa,
> Namibia, Southern Rhodesia (Zimbabwe) and
> the territories under Portuguese administra-
> tion in Africa in their legitimate struggle
> for freedom and independence. Committee II
> was to examine action on colonialism and
> apartheid in southern Africa: assessment of
> the present situation in various fields of
> action to be taken by the United Nations, and
> the Organizations of the United Nations system,
> by the Organization of African Unity, by non-
> governmental Organizations and by National
> liberation movements.[73]

Thus, the conference was geared to soliciting the opinions
and views of the leaders of the national liberation movements
of southern africa. The significance of the conference was
succinctly summarized by Elizabeth Landis:

> Although the conference was supposed to
> consider practical suggestions for "the
> support of the victims of colonialism
> and apartheid in southern Africa, "it was
> clear that most of the leaders were convin-
> ced that only force would change the situa-
> tion in the area. This was made clear in the
> Conference leadership positions given to
> the representatives of the liberation move-
> ments from the Portugese territories, as
> well as in other, more subtle ways."[74]

69

It appeared by 1972 and certainly by 1973 that most
African nations felt that the problem of decolonization
was beyond the scope of persuasion and that the only
language that the racist regimes of Portugal, Rhodesia,
and South Africa understood was the language of violence.

While the majority of African states continued to
give only material and technical support for the armed
struggle in southern Africa, through the Liberation Committee
of the Organization of African Unity, we must focus on the
strategies of certain individual African states, particularly
those states bordering on Angola, Mozambique, Rhodesia, and
South Africa, to gain a fuller sense of how some African
states attempted to expand their involvement in the liberation
movements.

Tanzania and Zambia are two African states that exemplify
the expanded military support of the national liberation movements in southern Africa. Because of the geographical proximity of these two states to the white-dominated regimes they
were able to offer meaningful assistance to the revolutionary
nationalists in creating fighting machines capable of challeng-
ing the defense forces of the white-dominated regimes of South
Africa. The precise role of the two countries has been described by Kenneth Grundy:

> Tanzania serves as a training ground for
> several hundred guerilla fighters involved
> in the colonial war against Portugese in
> Mozambique. The Congo (Kinshasha) has served
> the same function for the freedom fighters in
> Angola. In addition, Tanzania and Zambia have
> served as launching grounds for attacks by
> guerrilla fighters against the white-minority
> regimes of Rhodesia and Mozambique respectively.
> A Third crucial function which these states have
> served in the military efforts in southern Africa
> has been that of coordinator and a major channel
> for assistance to the movements from abroad. This
> has included channeling the international military
> and material support from China and the Soviet
> Union.[75]

The strong commitment of Zambia and Tanzania is to
intensify their support to the military efforts of the
national liberation movements of southern Africa can be
seen in a project the two countries jointly undertook
which would enable them to strengthen the military forces
of the liberation movements. Tanzania and Zambia sought
to complete the Tan-Zam railway so as to free land-locked
Zambia from its dependency on Rhodesia's railways to transport its foreign trade to the seas. The railway line has
come to be known as the Uhuru (Freedom) railway and its
significance has been explained in the following manner:

> The second and most important justification
> for the Tanzan is that it will help break
> Zambia's dependence on the white-ruled regimes
> of southern Africa and enable the Zambian
> Government to risk giving greater support to
> the liberation movements.[76]

The twenty-ninth U.N. session in 1974 witnessed African
nations going beyond the call for armed struggle to resolve
the problem of southern Africa. During this session African
nations recommended a further use of radical action to end
colonialism in southern Africa. They now challended the
credentials of South Africa or demanded the expulsion of that
nation from the World Organization. The address by Tanzania
represents this call for new action in the United Nations
in 1974:

> The Government of Tanzania is now convinced that
> the time has come for the United Nations to
> reconsider seriously its relationship with
> South Africa because of the racist policies of
> that country..
>
> ...We submit that every single day that
> apartheid South Africa continues to enjoy
> the rights and privileges of a member of this
> organization, while completely ignoring and vio-
> lating the corresponding obligations of member-
> ship, makes a mockery of the United Nations.
> For those reasons, Tanzania considers the con-
> tinued participation in our organization of the
> racists from Pretoria as a serious anomaly needing
> immdiate rectification by the expulsion of apar-
> theid South Africa from this organization.[77]

71

African nations attempted to carry through on this new strategy by attempting to have the credentials of South Africa rejected. The motion to reject the credentials was introduced in the Assembly by the representative of Senegal. The U.N. Credentials Committee was a nine member body made up of representatives from Senegal, Tanzania, Soviet Union, China, Phillippines, United States, Belgium, Costa Rica and Venezuela. The motion by Senegal was carried by a 5-4 vote. Those countries voting against South Africa were Senegal, Tanzania, Soviet Union, China, and the Philippines. The United States, Belgium and Costa Rica voted in favor of South Africa, while Venezuela abstained.

Dissatisfied with just having the credentials of South Africa suspended for the ongoing U.N. session in 1974, the African group of nations successfully won approval of a recommendation to have the question of the expulsion of South Africa from the United Nations considered by the Security Council, the body that is empowered to expel a member nation from the World Organization. Aware of the fact that the Western powers which possessed veto power in the Security Council, would use that power to prevent the expulsion of South Africa, African nations attempted this manuever because during this session the representative of the United Republic of Cameroon was chairman of the 15-member Security Council.

The three African nations which served on the Security Council during the 1974 session proposed the resolution to expel South Africa from the United Nations. Kenya, Mauritania, United Republic of Cameroon and Iraq in the Security Council offered the draft resolution:

The Security Council,

Having considered General Assembly resolution 3207 (XXIX) of 30 September 1974, in which the Assembly called upon Security Council "to review the relationship between the United Nations and South Africa in the light of the constant violation

by South Africa of the principles of the
Charter and the Universal Declaration of
Human Rights",

Having heard the statements of the
persons invited to address the Council on
this issue,

Taking note of the report of the special
committee on apartheid entitled "Violations
of the Charter of the United Nations and
resolutions of the General Assembly and the
Security Council by the South African regime"
(S/11537),

Mindful of the provisions of the Charter
concerning the rights and obligations of member
states particularly those of Articles, 1,2,6
55, and 56,

Recalling its resolutions 134 (1970), 181
(1963), 182 (1963), 190 (1964), 283 (1970), and
311 (1972), on the question of the policies of
apartheid of the Government of the Republic of
South Africa,

Reaffirming that the policies of apartheid
are contrary to the principles and purposes of
the charter and inconsistent with the provisions
of the Universal Declaration of Human Rights, as
well as with South Africa's obligations under
the Charter,

Recalling that the General Assembly and the
Security Council have more than once condemned
the South African Government for its persistent
refusal to abandon its policies of apartheid and
to abide by its obligations under the Charter as
called for by the Council and the Assembly,

Noting with concern South Africa's refusal
to withdraw its police and military forces, as
well as its civilian personnel from the mandated
territory of Namibia and to cooperate with the

United Nations in enabling the people of
Namibia as a whole to attain self-determination and independence,

Noting further that, in violation of the
pertinent resolutions of the Security Council,
particularly resolution 253 (1968) of 29 May
1968, South Africa has not only given support
to the illegal regime in Southern Rhodesia,
but also sent into that territory military
and police personnel for the purpose of stren-
gthening that regime in its attempt to impede
the exercise by the people of territory of
their inalienable rights,

Considering that effective measures should
be taken to resolve the present situation
arising out of the policies of apartheid, of
the Government of South Africa,

Recommends to the General Assembly the
immediate expulsion of South Africa from the
United Nations, in compliance with Article 6
of the Charter.[78]

But as expected the three western nations, the United States,
Britain and France used their vetoes to block the African
move to oust South Africa from the United Nations.

Still determined to take some radical, harsh, and punitive
action against South Africa despite the decision of the Security
Council, the African nations forced the issue of "suspension"
from the U.N. Assembly before that body. On November 13, 1974
the General Assembly voted to suspend South Africa's participation in that session. Th effect of the U.N. decision was that
South Africa was not permitted to take its seat, speak, make
proposals or vote. Although South Africa was not suspended from
membership in the World Organization, her privileges and
rights as a member nation were denied her at the twenty-ninth
session of the United Nations. South Africa chose to boycott
the thirtieth U.N. session in 1975.

The commitment of African nations to radical/militant
confrontation tactics on the issue of southern Africa or decolonization was reaffirmed in 1975 in the O.A.U. South Africa
was at that time calling for detente and dialogue with black

independent African nations. It was the belief of many
African nations that South Africa was making overtures
for dialogue with the deliberate purpose of dividing
and splitting African nations over the best manner of
resolving the problem of decolonization.

There were indications that South Africa was ob-
taining her desired goals when certain African countries
Liberia, Ivory Coast, Zaire, Central African Republic,
Zambia and Tanzania, were establishing contact with South
Africa by engaging in talks with her diplomats on the issue
of southern Africa.

In this context, the O.A.U. meeting in April 1975 at
Dar Es Salaam on southern Africa attempted to reaffirm the
solidarity of African nations toward South Africa. The
Declaration of Dar Es Salaam rejected dialogue between South
Africa and independent Black African nations over the issue
of decolonization, but called for dialogue between South
Africa and the indigenous Africans or leaders of the liberation movements of that country. The declaration also made
clear that any talks held between independent African
countries and South Africa would be solely for the purpose
of arranging for the process of transferring power to the
national majority of Africans in that country. Thus the
Declaration sought to reaffirm that African nations were
committed to militant radical techniques for resolving the
problem of decolonization.

Variation Among African Nations on Decolonization

We wish to examine variation in predilections for
certain techniques of influence on the issue of decolonization
according to geographical blocs, namely Central Africa,
East Africa, North Africa, West Africa, Southern Africa,
(Black Majority Regimes). For the list of African states
assigned to these various blocs see Table I-A.

Table IV shows a percentage breakdown of the various
techniques of influence favored by the geographical blocs of
African nations in the United Nations on the issue of decolonization for the years between 1967 and 1975. This data

75

PERCENTAGE OF AFRICAN NATIONS WITHIN EACH BLOC WHICH FAVORED EACH TYPE OF RECOMMENDATION IN THE UNITED NATIONS ON THE ISSUE OF DECOLONIZATION

TABLE – IV

	PERSUASION									ISOLATION								
	'67	'68	'69	'70	'71	'72	'73	'74	'75	'67	'68	'69	'70	'71	'72	'73	'74	'75
CENTRAL AFRICA	33	67	33	33	33	50	17	33	0	33	0	0	17	0	0	0	0	0
EAST AFRICA	67	67	17	0	50	0	0	17	0	17	33	67	33	0	33	0	17	0
NORTH AFRICA	50	17	17	0	0	33	17	0	17	0	33	0	0	17	0	0	0	17
WEST AFRICA	26	29	24	12	23	23	18	30	11	12	12	6	6	17	17	12	6	11
SOUTHERN AFRICA (Black Majority Regimes)	67	50	0	0	0	0	0	25	0	0	0	25	0	0	0	0	25	0

Percentages do not always total 100 because of rounding off

TABLE – IV CONTINUED

	MILITANT/RADICAL CONFRONTATION									NO RECOMMENDATION								
	'67	'68	'69	'70	'71	'72	'73	'74	'75	'67	'68	'69	'70	'71	'72	'73	'74	'75
CENTRAL AFRICA	0	0	17	0	0	33	50	33	17	33	33	67	50	67	17	33	33	67
EAST AFRICA	0	0	17	0	33	50	67	50	67	17	0	17	67	17		33	17	33
NORTH AFRICA	0	0	0	67	33	17	17	17	0	50	50	83	33	50	50	67	83	67
WEST AFRICA	6	0	18	12	12	45	30	24	21	56	59	53	71	50	12	41	41	58
SOUTHERN AFRICA (Black Majority Regimes)	0	0	0	0	0	0	25	25	0	33	50	75	100	100	75	75	25	100

Percentages do not always total 100 because of rounding off

77

compiled by computing the perentage total of each respective technique called for in debate by the various
countries constituting the various blocs.

Table V is a summary of the data presented in Table IV,
showing the cumulative percentage breakdown of the various
techniques of influence favored by the different geographical
blocs in the U.N. over the nine year period from 1967-1975 on
the issue of decolonization. The data reveals that the East
African nations tended to have the greatest predilection for
the use of techniques of militant/radical confrontation on
the issue of decolonization, with 32% of their total recommendations on the issue favoring this type of action.
The most conciliatory bloc on the issue of decolonization, in
the sense that it favored "persuasion" more often than any
other type of influence compared with the other blocs, was
the Central African bloc. 35% of this bloc's recommendations
on the issue called for the use of persuasion.

The data also clearly reveals that the most vociferous
bloc on the issue of decolonization in the U.N. was the
East African nations. As a bloc they had the lowest fre-
quency for making no recommendation on the issue in their
speeches. In 75% of their speeches, nations of this bloc
made recommendations on the issue of decolonization; this was
the highest percentage of all the blocs. The most silent
blocs on the issue were the North African states and the
Southern African (Black Regimes) states, these made the fewest
recommendations on the issue. The North African states made
no recommendation on the issue in 59% of their speeches for all
the U.N. sessions between 1967-1975 while the Southern African
(Black regimes) made no recommendation of action on the issue
in 57% of their speeches.

We see from Table V also that the geographical blocs
with the highest non-participation in the U.N. Debate on the
issue of decolonization were the North African and Black
Southern African nations. In the case of the North African
states the tendency to make speeches in the General Debate but
without specific recommendations of action on the issue of
decolonization can perhaps be explained by their lack of historical, cultural, and political cooperation in the past with
Sub-Sahara African states. The problem of decolonization while
historically experienced by North African and the Sub-Sahara
African states became one of the first political problems that

78

PERCENTAGE OF AFRICAN NATIONS WITHIN EACH BLOC WHICH FAVORED EACH TYPE OF RECOMMENDATION FROM 1967–1975 IN THE UNITED NATIONS ON THE ISSUE OF DECOLONIZATION

TABLE – V

GEOGRAPHICAL BLOC	PERSUASION	ISOLATION	MILITANT / RADICAL CONFRONTATION	NO RECOMMENDATION
CENTRAL AFRICA	33	6	17	44
EAST AFRICA	24	22	32	25
NORTH AFRICA	17	7	17	59
SOUTHERN AFRICA (Black Regimes)	19	6	6	70
WEST AFRICA	22	11	19	49

Percentages do not always total 100 because of rounding off

formed a basis for political coalescence between the two. Since it was a relatively new development for the two blocs to forego their historical aloofness, this may account for the tendency of North Africa not to be dogmatic on political issues that affect Sub-Sahara Africa.

The non-participation in the U.N. Debate of the Black Southern African states on the issue of decolonization appears to be explainable by the geographical and economic dependence of these black-majority regimes on South Africa and Rhodesia. These states, most of which are land locked, are dependent on South Africa and Rhodesia for land transport to export their various mineral and agricultural products in the international market. There exist a further economic dependence on the white minority regimes by the black southern African states in that many of their citizens earn their livelihoods by working in the mines of South Africa and Rhodesia. This is one of the chief sources of employment for the people of these states.

In this chapter we argued that in the U.N. General Debate Speeches between 1967 and 1975, African nations recommended three categories or types of influence on the issue of decolonization: persuasion, isolation and militant/radical confrontation.

When examining the degree of cohsion among African nations with respect to these various techniques, we found little overall cohesion. However, a plurality of support for persuasion can be shown in the period 1967-1971, while from 1972-1975, most African nations which spoke and made recommendations favored militant/radical confrontation techniques of influence on the issue of decolonization.

An equally important finding from our data in this chapter was that a high proportion (cumalitive 49%) of African nations refrained from making any recommendations at all on the issue of decolonization in the U.N. General Debate during the period of 1967-1975.

In examining variation along geographical blocs we found that the East African nations tended to have the greatest predilection for the use of militant/radical confrontation techniques of influence on the issue of decolonization, while the

Central African bloc of states appeared to be the most
conciliatory in terms of prefering more often to use
persuasion techniques of influence on the issue. The most
vociferous in debate on the issue were the East African states,
which made recommendations for the greatest number of U.N.
sessions between 1967-1975. The most silent on the issue
were the North African states, and the Southern African
(Black regimes) bloc, which made the fewest recommendations
on the issue.

   In the next chapter we will make a similar analysis of
influence by African nations on the issue of the Middle East
Crisis.

FOOTNOTES

38. Ibid.

39. Ibid. pg. 157-158-

40. Ibid., 157-58

41. Official Records of the General Assembly, Fifteenth Session. Supplement No. 16, p. 66-67.

42. United Nations General Assembly Official Records, Supplement 17, 16th Session (A/5100), pg. 65.

43. U.N. Department of Political and Security Affairs, Review of United Nations Consideration of Apartheid, New York, 1974, p.1.

44. Ibid.

45. Ibid.

46. Ibid.

47. John Norris, An Examination of the Sanctions That Have Been Imposed On the Republic of South Africanand Rhodesia Masters Thesis, University of Illinois (Urbana, Illinois, 1973) pg.78

48, Ibid., p. 78-79

49. Ibid, p. 77.

50. Colin Legum, The United Nations and Southern Africa (Britain, 1974), pg. 20.

51. Ibid.

52. United Nations Document A/PV. 1587, October 11, 1967.

53. Colin Legum, Africa Contemporary Record, (London, 1970), pg. 41-42.

54. United Nations Document A/PV. 1780, October 6, 1969.

55. United Nations Document A/PV. 1780, October 15, 1970.

56. United Nations Document A/PV. 1848, September 24, 1970.

57. New York Times, February 8, 1970, pg. 7.

58. Ibid.
59. New York Times, February 17, 1970, pg. 3
60. Ibid.

61. Ibid.

62. New York Times, February 13, 1970, pg. 7.

63. New York Times, July 11, 1971, pg. 6.

64. Ibid.

65. New York Times, June 24, 1971, pg. 15.

66. New York Times, April 29, 1971, pg. 1.

67. New York Times, January 28, 1964, pg. 36.

68. New York Times, May 23, 1975, pg. 6.

69. New York Times, May 23, 1975, pg. 45.

70. United Nations Document, A/PV. 2127, September 25, 1973.

71. V. Zdenek Cervenka, "Major Policy Shifts In The Organization of African Unity", in K. Ingham, ed., Foreign Relations of African States (Butterworths, 1974) pg. 338.

72. Ibid., pg. 339

73. U.N. Document A/9061 (May 7, 1973), pg. 13.

74. Elizabeth S. L ndis, "Notes on The   Conference On Southern Africa," Africa Today, Vol. 20, No. 2, Spring 1973, pg. 60.

75. Kenneth W. Grundy, "Host Countries and the Southern African Liberation Struggle," Africa Quarterly, Vol. 10, 1971, pg. 21.

76. Martin Bailey, "Tanzania and China," African Affairs, Vol. 74, No. 294, January 1975, pg. 45.

77. United Nations Document, A/PV. 2250, Oct, 1, 1974.

78. United Nations Document S/11543, October 24, 1974.

CHAPTER IV

AFRICA AND THE MIDDLE EAST CRISIS: A
CASE STUDY OF INFLUENCE IN THE UNITED NATIONS

The purpose of this chapter is to examine the techniques of influence favored by African nations in the United
Nations on the issue of the Middle East Crisis. This will
be done specifically by (1) examining relevant historical
and foreign policy actions by African nations; (2) identifying the various techniques as expressed in the U.N.
General Debate; (3) determining the percentages of African
nations favoring the use of the various techniques and
(4) examining variation among African nations in the U.N.
along geographical blocs as to their predilections for the
various techniques.

The Middle East Crisis, as already established in
Chapter II, was the issue of second greatest concern to
African nations in the U.N. between 1967-1975. Our analysis
of the U.N. Debate sessions for the nine year period showed
that the Middle East Crisis was raised by an overall average
of 90% of African nations addressing the body.

We will proceed first by examining the historical background of the Middle East Crisis. The Arab nations have con-
stantly challenged and opposed the existence of Israel since
its establishment in 1948. This controversial issue has
erupted into four wars, in 1948, 1956, 1967 and 1973 between
Arab nations and the state of Israel. The circumstances
surrounding the establishment of Israel should briefly be
explored for clearer understanding of the Middle East crisis
and the United Nation's role in it.

Palestine was a part of the Ottoman empire before W.W.I.
Turkey fought on the side of Germany in World War I and as a
result of Germany's defeat, Palestine was given as a mandate
territory to Britain by the League of Nations in 1922. At
the beginning of the mandate years the Arab population of
Palestine was 400,000 Arabs and only 100,000 Jews. With the
ascendancy of Nazi rule in Germany during the 1930's, Jewish
migration to Palestine increased significantly. Jewish

migration had also been inspired by the Balfour Declaration
of November 2, 1917. The Balfour Declaration was a statement
of support for the establishment of a Jewish state. The
Declaration designated Palestine as the place for the
national home for the Jewish people. The Balfour Declaration
was interpreted by the Jewish people ". .as a contract binding victorious Britain to support the foundation of a Jewish
state on Jewish land liberated from a foreign enemy."[79] By
this time there had developed a Zionist or Jewish nationalist
movement which aimed at creating Palestine as a Jewish state
and subsequently encouraged Jewish migration from the diaspora
to Palestine.

With the heavy immigration and influx of Jews to
Palestine as a result of Zionism and the rise of Hitler, the
Arab population felt threatened. The Arabs began to retaliate
with sporadic armed attacks against the Jewish community of
Palestine. Thus evolved the conflict between Arabs and Jews
which was to continue only to levels of greater intensity.
Britain proved incapable of erasing the tension and violence
that was erupting between the Arabs and Jews of Palestine.
As a result "in February, 1947 the British declared the
Mandate 'Unworkable' and laid the problem of the future of
Palestine in the lap of the United Nations."[80]

The United Nations appointed a Special Committee on
Palestine to study and make recommendations on the Palestine
problem. The United Nations Special Committee on Palestine
(UNSCOP), composed of representatives from eleven countries,
conducted an investigation by travelling to the Middle East
and soliciting testimony from Britain, Jews, and Arabs. After
four months of investigating the Palestine problem the UNSCOP:

> ...recommended that Palestine be partitioned
> into independent Jewish and Arab states, that
> Jerusalem be internationalized under a United

Nations trusteeship, and that the
three areas be linked in an economic union.[81]

On November 29, 1947, the General Assembly of the United
Nations adopted a resolution proposing the partition of
Palestine into two states, one Jewish and one Arab. The
resolution called for the British Mandate to end in May, 1948.

The Jewish community accepted the proposed U.N. partition of Palestine. However, the Arab nations of the
Middle East rejected the proposal. The response of the
Arab nations to the proposal was that this action was
beyond the scope of the United Nation's charter, and that
it was an unjust and inequitable solution. Arab leaders
verbalized their opposition to the proposal and committed
themselves to preventing it from being carried out.

The UNSCOP reported to the Security Council in February
1948 that the partition of Palestine was not being accomplished because of the failure of British administrators
to cooperate and because "...powerful Arab interests, both
inside and outside Palestine, are defying the resolution
of the General Assembly and are engaged in a deliberate effort to alter by force the settlement envisaged therein."[82]
Arab opposition to the partition of Palestine resulted in an
armed conflict in the Middle East. Arabs carried out an
armed invasion into Palestine on January 9, 1948. This was
the beginnings of the 1948 war in the Middle East over the
creation of the State of Israel. During the armed invasion
when British rule ended on May 14, 1948, the Jewish community
of Palestine proclaimed the independent Jewish nation to be
called Israel.[83] The Jewish community already had established
a provisional government.

Six hours after the Jewish proclamation of Israel, the
Arab nations unleashed full-scale war against Israel with
the objective of destroying her. Armies from Egypt, Jordan,
Syria, Lebanon, Iraq with contingents from Saudi Arabia and
Yemen attacked Israel from the north, south and east. The
United Nations negotiated a ceasefire in June when the Arab

nations realized that victory for them was not going to be easy or fast. The truce was broken by both sides and the hostilities resumed. The final operations of the war were staged in January, 1949. The war resulted in Armistice Agreements. These agreements intended to be temporary measures, to be supplanted by permanent peace treaties. The Armistice agreements were reached under the auspices of the United Nations between January and July of 1949. These agreements were signed by Egypt, Lebanon, Jordan and Syria.

The Armistice Agreements were merely a number of general principles which were to lead to a permanent peace treaty. They merely committed Israel and Arab nations to the principles of not engaging in armed attack against each other and to eliminate the threat to peace in the Middle East by facilitating a transition to permanent peace agreements. But the fact is that the Armistice Agreements never lead to the conclusion of a permanent peace treaty.

The United Nations pursued another course of action to seek peace between Israel and her Arab neighbors. It established a Palestine Conciliation Commission with the objective of finding a ground upon which a permanent peace settlement could be established. The commission consisted of three nations, the United States, France and Turkey. Arab nations stifled the ability of the Commission to achieve its aim by refusing to meet with the representatives of Israel. Thus, the commission was forced to hold separate negotiating meetings with the Arabs and Israel. The result was that it was not able to achieve a peace treaty between Arab nations and Israel.

Although the objective of the Arab nations in the 1948-1949 war was not realized, Egypt did gain some territory, the Gaza strip. Lebanon was the only Arab nation to lose territory but this was only temporary until the Israelis agreed to give back the southern part of Lebanon it occupied in the Armistice Agreements. Because of the nature in which this round of hostilities ended in terms of agreements reached

it was inevitable that the future hostilities between
Israel and Arab nations would erupt.

The second outbreak of war between Arab nations and
Israel occured in 1956. This was was inevitable because of
the violatile situation left in the Middle East from the
inability of the U.N. to get a permanent peace treaty between
the Arab states and Israel. In other words, each side felt
that the other intended to attack it sometime in the future.
This military paranoia, therefore, inevitably erupted into
another war in 1956. Israel launched the military offensive
in 1956 because she felt it necessary to strike first before
the Arab nations did since she had reason to belive that
the Arab world was preparing to do so.

Israel's 1956 military campaign against Arab nations was
triggered by several specific factors. During the first
war, Egypt and Syria were increasing their military stock-
piles with supplies and assistance from the Soviet Union.
Prior to this build-up, which began around 1953, the balance of
arms between Israel and her Arab neighbors, was about even.
However, by 1956 the balance of arms was significantly tilted
in favor of the Arab nations. In addition to this was the
fact that Egypt, Syria, and Jordan had established a joint
military command. As a result of these factors, Israel gen-
uinely interpreted them as indications that the Arab nations
were preparing to attack her again.

Subsequently, the Prime Minister of Israel gained approval
from the Israeli cabinet for military action in light of
these facts in self-defense of Israel. Operation Kaddish as
this military offensive was called had as its objective to
capture the Sinai Peninsula, the Egyptian positions controlling
the Strait of Tiran, and to bring about the collapse of the
organized Egyptian forces.

Operation Kaddish was launched on October 29, 1956, and
after eight days the campaign proved militarily successful.

> ...freedom on shipping for Israeli vessels
> through the Strait of Tiran and the Gulf
> of Agaba was restored, Gasa Strip fedayien
> bases (guerillas) were destroyed; and the
> threat of a coordinated Egyptian-Jordanian-
> Syrian attack on Israel was neutralized...[84]

88

Despite the fact that the U.N. was able to get Israel and the Arab world to enter these agreements, peace was not secure in the Middle East because Israel had no guarantee that Egypt would live up to her promises made to a third party, the United Nations.

The third outbreak of war between Israel and Arab nations was to occur about ten years later in 1967. The crisis which led to this outbreak began when Egypt in mid-May of 1967 requested that the U.N. Emergency Forces of 4,000 men be removed from the Egypt-Israeli armistice line and the Strait of Tiran. These forces were established ten years after the 1956 war. The U.N. Secretary General yielded to Egypt's request convinced that Egypt was exercising her sovereign rights. Egypt subsequently replaced the U.N. forces with her troops along the armistice lines and the Sinai Peninsula. Egypt followed this action by declaring that she was prepared to fight in case of an Israeli attack on any Arab state.

Egypt was to take one other measure which heightened the tension between Israel and herself: "... the UAR government. By November 5, Israel was in command of the Strait of Tiran, the Egyptian governor-general of the Gaza strip surrendere this territory to her and the Sinai Peninsula was in her control. By November 6, when United Nations cease-fire orders arrived, the Kaddish operation had realized its military objectives.

Britain assumed a role of neutrality in Operation Kaddish and the 1956 War. The only western nation to involve itself in the war by actually selling arms to Israel was France. The United States and Britain were unwilling to sell defensive arms to Israel in 1956 despite the fact that Egypt was receiving arms from communist nations.

Israel accepted the U.N. call for a cease fire while she rejected its demand for an unconditional, immediate withdrawal. When the Secretary General of the U.N., Dag Hammarskjold negotiated settlement between Israel and the Arab nations because Egypt refused to negotiate directly with Israel,

Israel agreed to withdraw her forces behind the old
armistice lines on the condition that they would be
replaced by international emergency forces. It was
four and a half months later when Israel withdrew her
forces from the newly occupied territory and at the
same time they were replaced by the United Nations
Emergency Forces (UNEF). Thus, the UNEF were placed in
the Gaza Strip, the Sinai Peninsula and at the Strait
of Tiran. The Sinai campaign despite this arrangement
accomplished three things for Israel: declared the
closure of the Strait of Tiran to all shipping to and
from Israel."[85] The Israeli response to this action
was that it declared the closure of the Strait to be a
belligerent act. In addition, if no one acted to remove
the blockade, she, Israel herself, would. Two days after
Israel relayed this message, Egypt entered into a defense
pact with Jordan. Israeli high officials then decided
that war was necessary.

The war lasted for six days, beginning June 5. Israeli
air attacks virtually destroyed the air forces of Egypt,
Jordan and Syria. "Isralei ground forces then invaded
Egypt, Jordan and Syria successively, and by the end of
the week had reached the Suex Canal, the Jordan River and
the city of El Quneitra in southwestern Syria."[86] When
the six day war ended, Israel occupied territory over four
times the size of itself, entailing a population of over a
million Arabs. Israel incorporated the city of Jerusalem
into its own territory after the war.

The U.N. Security Council met in emergency session
throughout the crisis period of the Middle East War. The
Council, however, was so decided that it was unable to take
action. The Security Council was only able to pass resolutions calling for a ceasefire which was honored after
Israel was satisfied with her military victories and the
Arab nations were convinced that they were defenseless
against Israel.

The fourth Arab-Israeli outbreak occured in 1973. The
cause of the Yom Kippur War in 1973 has been attributed to
the conscious decision of President Anwar Sadat of Egypt.

Having succeeded President Nasser upon his death in 1970
Sadat was pressured to reassure Arabs that his position
toward Israel would be conciliatory. Sadat was therefore
under pressure to break the "no war-no peace" state of
the Israel-Arab conflict.

Sadat responded to these pressures by developing a
military strategy between Syria and Egypt to cross the
Suez Canal in an armed attack against Israel. The Yom
Kippur War began when a Syrian military attack took place
in the Golan Heights on October 6, 1973. This was to
be the heaviest fighting in the Middle East since the
1967 war erupted.

The United Nations Secrutiy Council immediately convened
and was able to bring a cease fire into effect on November 14,
1973 between Egypt and Syria. The U.N. Security Council
established peace-keeping forces to insure the cease fire agr
agreement between Arab and Israeli forces.

The series of events of the Yom Kippur War were to cul-
minate when both Egypt, Syria and Israel agreed to a peace
conference in Geneva on December 21, 1973 to reach a permanent
settlement that would avoid another Middle East War.

The United Nations and the Middle East Crisis

The role of the United Nations in the Middle East Crisis,
as indicated by the above accounts of each of the Arab-
Israeli Wars,had mainly been that of condemnations and of
obtaining cease-fire agreements after an immediate outbreak.

The Security Council has been the body of the United
Nations that has been responsible for dealing with the
Arab-Israeli outbreaks, according to its Charter obligations.

The only definitive policy decision reached by the U.N.
on the Middle East Crisi is embodied in Resoliton 242 (1967)
of the Security Council, in which the United Nations
declared the inadmissibility of acquiring territory by war
and called for the guarantee of political and territorial

independence of every state in the Middle East area.
African Nations voiced strong support of this resolution.

African Influence on Middle East Crisis; 1967 - 1975

Before we proceed to outline the strategies of influence
favored by African nations on the issue of the Middle East
Crisis we must more explicitly convey the African perception
of this issue in 1967.

From the policy positions expressed by African nations
in the U.N. General Debate it appears that African nations
perceived the problem of the Middle East as one of violation
of the principle of "territorial integrity." By this term
African nations attached the same meaning as the Security
Council Resolution 242 (1967)did. African nations throughout
the period between 1967-1975 expressed support of this
resolution in interpreting the problem and events of the
Middle East. The resolution states that the Security Council,

> Emphasizing the inadmissibility of the
> acquisition of territory by war and the
> need to work for a just and lasting peace
> in which every state in the area can live
> in security....
>
> 1. Affirms that the fulfillment of Charter
>   principles requires the establishment of a
>   just and lasting peace in the Middle East
>   which should include the application of both
>   the following principles:
>
>   (i) withdrawal of Israel armed forces from
>   territories occupied in the recent con-
>   flict;
>
>   (ii) termination of all claims or states of
>   belligerency and respect for and acknow-
>   ledgement of the sovereignty, territorial
>   integrity and political independence of
>   every state in the area and their right

92

INFLUENCE TECHNIQUES FAVORED BY AFRICAN NATIONS IN THE UNITED NATIONS ON THE ISSUE OF THE MIDDLE EAST CRISIS

TABLE – VI

COUNTRY	'67	'68	'69	'70	'71	'72	'73	'74	'75
Algeria	NR	NS	NR	MRC	P	NO	I	NR	NR
Botswana	P	ND	ND	NS	NS	NS	NS	NR	NS
Burundi	NR	P	P	NS	NS	NR	P	MRC	NS
Cameroon	P	P	NS	ND	P	P	NS	P	NR
Central African Republic	NS	NS	ND	NS	P	P	ND	NR	NS
Chad	P	P	P	NS	P	NR	NS	NR	NR
Congo (Brazzaville)	P	NS	NR	P	P	ND	I	NR	NR
Dahomey	NS	NS	NS	NS	P	P	NR	P	P
Ethiopia	P	P	P	NS	P	P	NR	NR	NS
Equatorial Guinea	-	NS	P	NS	P	NS	ND	NR	NR
Gabon	P	NR	P	NS	P	P	P	ND	ND
Gambia	NR	P	NS	P	NS	ND	NS	NR	NS
Ghana	P	P	NS	P	NR	NR	NR	P	P
Guinea	NS	P	P	NR	P	NR	NR	NS	

Key --
ND=No Discussion   -=Non Member of U.N.   MRC=Militant
NR=No Recommendation NS=No Speech I=Isolation P=Persuasian Radical
Confrontation

TABLE – VI CONTINUED

	'67	'68	'69	'70	'71	'72	'73	'74	'75
Ivory Coast	NS	NS	NR	NS	P	P	NS	P	NS
Kenya	P	P	P	P	P	NR	P	P	P
Lesotho	NR	P	NS	NS	NS	NS	MRC	NR	P
Liberia	P	NR	NR	P	P	P	P	P	NR
Libya	NR	NR	NR	I	NR	ND	MRC	MRC	NR
Madagascar	P	P	NS	ND	P	NR	NR	NS	NR
Malawi	P	P	NS	NS	P	P	NS	NS	NS
Mali	NR	NS	NR	NS	P	NR	NR	NR	NR
Mauritania	NR	NR	MRC	NS	P	P	NR	MRC	NR
Morocco	P	P	P	P	P	NR	NR	MRC	NR
Niger	ND	NS	NS	NS	P	P	I	NR	NS
Nigeria	NR	P	P	NS	P	P	NR	NR	P
People's Republic of Mozambique	–	–	–	–	–	–	–	–	P
Republic of Cape Verde	–	–	–	–	–	–	–	–	NS

94

TABLE – VI CONTINUED

	'67	'68	'69	'70	'71	'72	'73	'74	'75
Rwanda	P	P	P	P	P	P	P	NR	P
Senegal	P	P	P	NS	ND	P	NR	P	NR
Sierra Leone	P	P	P	P	P	P	NR	NR	P
Somalia	P	P	I	NR	P	NR	I	NS	MRC
Sudan	NR	NR	NR	NR	NR	NR	NR	NS	NR
Swaziland	-	NS	NR	NS	NS	NS	NS	P	NS
Togo	P	NR	NS	P	P	P	NS	P	P
Tunisia	NR	P	P	P	NR	NR	NR	MRC	P
Uganda	-	P	NR	NS	P	ND	NS	NR	MRC
United Arab Republic	P	P	P	P	P	P	NR	MRC	NS
United Republic of Tanzania	P	P	P	NS	NR	P	NR	MRC	MRC
Upper Volta	P	NS	P	P	P	P	NR	P	NR
Zaire	P	P	P	NS	NS	NR	I	NR	I
Zambia	NR	P	P	P	P	P	NR	P	NR

*Not listed in a table is Democratic Republic of SAO Tome and Principe, which didn't gain membership to U.N. until 1975 at which time she made no recommendation on the issue in the U.N. Debate.

95

PERCENTAGE BREAKDOWN OF VARIOUS ACTIONS RECOMMENDED BY AFRICAN NATIONS ON THE ISSUE OF THE MIDDLE EAST CRISIS IN THE UNITED NATIONS

TABLE - VII

		1967	1968	1969	1970	1971	1972	1973	1974	1975
PERSUASION	Negotiation	39	45	36	33	65	45	13	27	23
	Appeal	29	12	7	2	2	5	0	0	0
	Total	58	57	43	35	67	50	13	27	23
ISOLATION		0	0	2	3	0	0	13	0	2
MILITANT/RADICAL CONFRONTATION	Support Armed Struggle	0	0	2	3	0	0	5	18	3
	Expulsion From United Nations	0	0	0	0	0	0	0	0	4
	Total	0	0	2	3	0	0	5	18	7
NO ACTION RECOMMENDED		42	43	53	60	33	50	70	55	70

to live in peace within secure and
recognized boundaries free from
threats or acts of force....[87]

In accord with this interpretation of the principle
of "territorial integrity," African nations favored the
withdrawal of Israel to her boundaries before 1967. This
position was maintained consistently by African nations which
spoke in the U.N. General Debate on the issue of the Middle
East Crisis between 1967-1975.

Table VI contains a notation of the various techniques
of influence favored by all African nations on the issue of
the Middle East Crisis for each U.N. session between 1967-
1975. If a nation made no recommendation on the issue, or
did not make a speech in the Debate at all, or simply did not
discuss the Middle East Crisis in their speech before debate,
this is so indicated in the table.* Techniques are again
categorized, as in the previous chapter, in the three types:
Persuasion (P) Isolation, Militant/radical/confrontaion (MRC).

Table VII summarized the data in Table VI, showing the
percentage of African nations that favored each type of
techniques of influence. The data reveals primarily that
there was a very high percentage of African nations which did not
recommend any type of action on this issue in the U.N. General
Debates between 1967-1975. For five of the nine sessions of
least 50% or more of all African nations made no recommendation
of any type of action on the problem; while at the remaining
four sessions the proportion of African nations which remained
silent was between 33-43%. The overall percentage of African
nations which made no recommendation of any type of action on
the Middle East Crisis in the U. N. General Debates between
1967 and 1975 was 53%.

97

*Appendix II contains a complete analysis of the position and
types of action recommended by all African nations in the U.N.
Debates between 1967-1975 on the Middle East Crisis. The
data and tables throughout this chapter are compiled from the
data contained in Appendix II.

Persuasion

Table VII further reveals that a majority of African
nations which did speak on this issue in the U.N. General
Debate favored the use of persuasion as a means of resolving the
Middle East Crisis for every year between 1967-1975 except
1973. The overall percentage of African nations calling for
the use of persuasion techniques as a means for resolving
the Middle East Crisis was 41% between the nine years from
1967 to 1975, or 85% of those who made some recommendation
on the issue.

This position was also visible outside the United Nations
General Debate. African nations expressed their hope, faith
and support of the appointment of Ambassador Gunard Jarring
in 1967 as the special representative of the U.N. to mediate
between Israel and the Arab nations. The creation of the
Jarring Mission was a part of Resolution 242 (1967) of the
U.N. Security Council. Ambassador Jarring shuttled between
the capitals of the Middle East hoping to negotiate a settlement between Israel and her Arab neighbors. But the Jarring
mission, six months after receiving its charge, had proved
a failure, unable to realize its objective in the Middle East.

The Jarring mission resulted in a stalemate because
each of the Arab countries and Israel selected the parts of
resolution 242 which it favored as the major priorities requiring immediate implementation. Ambassador Jarring was
charged with negotiating a settlement in the Middle East
based on the principles of Resolution 242 (1967). The Arab
nations gave priority to the principle which calls for the
withdrawal of Israel's armed forces from the Arab territories
it occupied as a result of the conflict. Israel laid emphasis on the clause of the resolution calling for the acknowledgement of the sovereignty , territorial integrity and
political independence of every state in the area.

Despite Jarring's failure African nations did not abandon support of the strategy of persuasion as the means of in-

98

fluencing the issue of the Middle East Crisis. In their U.N. Debate Speeches in 1970, they supported the negotiation efforts by the U.S. Secretary of State William Rogers. This negotiation initiative, known as the "Rogers Plan" was simply an attempt to realize the Jarring principles. With the United States as mediator, the Rogers Plan called for discussions be- tween Israel and Arab nations that would lead to an agreed upon, just, and lasting peace based on the mutural acknowledgement by the Arab nations of the sovereignly and territorial integrity of Israel and Israeli with- drawal from the territories it occupied in the 1967 War. The Rogers Plan was also unsuccessful. And it was in 1971 that African nations embarked upon their own negotiation inititative in the Middle East Crisis.

This came about as a result of a decision at the eighth summit meeting of the Organization of African Unity in 1971. In Order to appease the North African states of Egypt, Libya, and others with Arab cultural links, the O.A.U. decided to play a more active role in the Middle East Crisis. Prior to 1971 the African nations had only expressed support for U.N. resolutions calling for a just settlement. The chairman of the O.A.U., Kenneth Kaunda "...proposed that Africa should appoint from among its own leaders 'Ten Wise Men' to attempt what the big powers has so far failed to do in helping to bring peace to the Middle East."[88] The President of Kenya, Ivory Coast, Tanzania, Senegal, Zaire, Cameroon, Liberia, Mauritania, the Emperor of Ethipia, and the head of the Military Government of Nigeria, were appointed to comprise the mediation team.

The African mediators defined their mandate as gaining acceptance from Israel and the Arab nations "...to resume indirect negotiations under the auspices of Dr. Jarring and within the terms of Resolution 242 in order to reach a peace agreement."[89] Therefore, the African initiative in the Middle East Crisis was merely an attempt to persuade Israel and the Arab nations to accept the settlement proposals of the United Nations. This was made clear by the African

99

mediators after their first round of talks with Egyptian and Israeli leaders. In a memorandum written by the 'Ten Wise Men' at a meeting following their first round of talks with Israel and Egypt in November 1971, it was clear that:

> ...the hopes for peace which African states
> share with the International Community are
> based precisely on the acceptance by Egypt
> and by Israel of Resolution 242, and supported
> Ambassador Jarring as a mediator, and (seek)   90
> ...to assist him in implementing Resolution 242.

The mediation and negotiation initiative of African nations in the Middle East Crisis however did not meet with the success anticipated by the African nations. The final report of the African negotiation in the Middle East was[91] submitted to the Chairman of OAU and the United Nations. This report was an analysis of the Middle East Crisis in terms of identifying the barriers which blocked a final settlement between Israel and the Arab nations.

African nations reported that while both Israel and the Arab nations reaffirmed the principles for a settlement based on the Security Council Resolution 242, there were two points which prevented a peace agreement. The first barrier was Egypt's preoccupation with the withdrawal of Israel from all occupied territories of the June 1967 War. African nations noted that once this occured, Egypt would be ready to conclude a permanent peace agreement with Israel and ensure Israel's access to the Suez Canal and the Strait of Tiran. The second and perhaps the most difficult barrier, the African report noted, was Israel's intransigence in accepting the creation of "...machinery to ensure adequate security guarantees without the annexation of territories."[92] Thus, the negotiation initiative of the African nations in the Middle East Crisis came to an end with no success.

African nations expressed disappointment at what they saw as Israel's intransigence on the issue. After the mission failed, they turned to other techniques in their attempts to influence the Middle East Crisis.

Isolation

In 1973, some African nations began a new attempt to influnce the Middle East Crisis. As pointed out earlier the African nations which spoke in the U.N. General Debate on this issue favored persuasion techniques of influence for every year between 1967-1975, except for one, 1973. As Table VII shows, African nations that spoke in that year were evenly divided between persuasion and isolation techques of influence. While 70% of all African nations refrained from making any recommendation, 13% recommended persuasion, 13% recommended isolation techniques and 5% recommended militant/radical confrontation techniques. Obviously there was no consensus, nor any plurality of support for any particular type of influence on 1973 on the issue of the Middle East Crisis.

Thus, our data does not confirm isolation as a distinct stage of influence on the issue of the Middle East Crisis. The overall average percent of African nations supporting the use of isolation techniques of influence on the Middle East Crisis was a mere 2%.

However, it appears from foreign policy action background material that "Isolation" was a variable technique of influence which was used in 1973 on the Middle East Crisis, a result of pressure exerted on Black African states from North African states in the O.A.U.

In 1973 African nations began to use deprivations against Israel, in particular, by severing diplomatic relations with her. In May of 1972, Israel had had 31 diplomatic missions in black Africa; a year and a half later, in November 1973, only five black African nations granted diplomatic recognition to Israel. Of course, the North African countries with Arab-Muslim cultural links such as Libya, Algeria, Tunisia, etc,.

101

had not had diplimatic relations with Israel, but the
sub-Sahara black African states had maintained diplomatic recognition of Israel since their independence.

The severance of diplomatic relations after 1973
in protest over the Israeli occupation of Arab territories
was announced by African nations in the U.N., for example,
in the statement by Equatorial Guinea:

> ...at the twenty-eight session of the
> General Assembly, from this rostrum we
> gave public notice of the breaking off
> of our diplomatic relations with the
> Zionist state of Israel becasue of its
> policy óf imperialist annexation; and
> while that state continues to occupy
> independent Arab territories and to
> ignore the rights of the Palestinian
> peoples, the Government of the Republic of
> Equatorial Guniea will not reconsider its
> position.[93]

Uganda observed in the U.N. at the same session:

> In 1972 Uganda was the first African Country
> to sever relations with Israel, thereby
> spearheading the move which successfully
> isolated the Zionist State from recognition
> by African countries.[94]

In 1973, at the tenth meeting of the Organization of African
Unity, African states were pressured by the Arab states to
draft a "political declaration" on the issue of the Middle
East Crisis. At this meeting "...Arab delegates wanted a
far stronger show of support for their stand against Israel
from black Africans than Blacks are willing to give."[95]
The meeting resulted in a debate so heated that it almost
threatened the survival of the organization.

Arab delegates chose this meeting to force the issue of
the organization's position on Israel because as one observer
aptly noted:

> ...In the past the Arabs had sought to trade
> their support of the liberation movements
> against South Africa and Portugal - for black
> African support against Israel. The Arabs
> always felt they got the worst of the deal -
> and they did.[96]

The Arab delegates seized this opportunity to force a more
definite African position toward Israel because it had already, prior to the O.A.U. meeting, won the support of six
black African states as a result of an envoy to black Africa
by Libyan delegates. This was one of the most sensitive
issues ever to confront the 42-member Organization of African
Unity, an amalgamation of Arab and black African states.

It was particularly sensitive issue because Israel
had been an important source of technical aid to black African
states, particularly in the field of agriculture. Up to
1973 black Africa had not taken offensive steps which would
identify them necessarily with the Arab cause in the Middle
East Crisis. Africa had merely supported mediation attempts
in the Arab-Israeli conflict. But the lobby of the
Arab-related African states forced the O.A.U. to make its
stand clear in regard to Israel. No longer were they satisfied with black Africa merely passing resolutions condemning
Israel and calling for a return of the lands taken during the
1967 war.

In their call for a stronger stand against Israel, the
Arab delegates specifically called for black Africa to break
diplomatic relations with Israel. They convinced black African
states that the Middle East Crisis was not just a problem of
aggression but one of imperialism and racism. The President of
Algeria, Houari Boumediene in an address to the African states
on this occasion noted:

> Africa cannot adopt one attitude toward
> racism in South Africa and a different
> one toward Zionism in North Africa.[97]

Mr. Boumediene then urged the complete breaking or suspension
of relations with Israel by the black African states.

103

The move to define the Arab cause to be the same as the African cause of decolonization of southern Africa was developed further by the President of Egypt, Anwar Sadat. Sadat, speaking as one of the principal African nations involved directly in the middle East Crisis told the African states:

> There is aggression in Africa and not just in one part of Africa. The aggression is one aspect of a plot aimed at draining the potential of this continent. This happens to be the northern tip of the plot. It is countered by aggression and pressure in the south, demonstrated by vestiges of imperialism and racial discrimination. We must realize that if such a besiegement of the continent were allowed to proceed it would eventually paralyze our progress, consume our strength and prevent us from harnessing our potential for the welfare of Africa."[98]

But the Arab states were not the only ones to identify the Middle East Crisis as the same as that of southern Africa. One black African state joined in the call for the severing relations with Israel based on the same argument. President Idi Amin of Uganda, in his address to African states on the same occasion observed that:

> "...Israel is no different from South Africa and Portugal. They took the Palestinians' land - the same tactics as in Rhodesia.[99]

Therefore "isolation" as a technique of influence was used by African nations as a result of pressure in the O.A.U. in 1973.

104

Militant/Radical Confrontation

Table VII reveals that only for five of the nine
U.N. sessions between 1967-1975 was there support for
militant/radical confrontation techniques of influence in the
Middle East Crisis. The overall average proportion of
African nations that favored the use of militant/radical
confrontation techniques on the Middle East Crisis was only 4%
However, in two of the five U.N. sessions there was some
noteworthy support by African nations in the U.N. for militant/
radical confrontation techniques, namely in 1974 and 1975. In
these two years, support by African nations for these techniques
was 18% and 7% respectively.

Although during these two years the plurality of support by African nations in the U.N. General Debate was still
for persuasion, the proceeding of the U.N. sessions show that
during this period African nations supported Arab-led unprecedented actions against Israel. In doing so, it appears that
African nations may have been reciprocating for the support
Arab nations had given to them in the past on the issue of
decolonization.

At the 1974 United Nations Assembly Session African nations
gave support for the presidency of the U.N. General Assembly
to Abdelaziz Bouteflika, the foreign minister of Algeria, who
was known to advocate a militant stance toward Israel. The
presidency of the United Nations by tradition rotates to
a different regional candidate each year. The choice by the
African bloc was Bouteflika, a man who had an established history of involvement in Arab politics. Many nations of the U.N.
feared that Bouteflika would be partisan in favor of the third
world countries in presiding over the Assembly. Bouteflika,
in giving his acceptance speech as the newly elected President
of the U.N., delivered a militant speech advocating self-
determination for Palestinians. Upon his assumption of office,
the Algerian Foreign Minister was to use his power as President
of the U.N. Assembly to impose radical measures against Israel
and to lend support to Arab-led moves directed against her.

105

One of the first radical moves taken aginst Israel in the U,N. at the twenty-ninth or 1974 session was to have "the Palestinian question" debated in the U.N.[100] This was a new development; the issue of Palestinians had always been discussed as a part of and ur⌐⌐⌐ the "Middle East problems" in previous General Assembly sessions.

The move to have a full debate on Palestinians was Arab-African led, and was obviously a tactic aimed at isolating Israel. The request ⌐⌐⌐ the inclusion of this topic on the agenda came from all twenty Arab nations in the world organization and many African and communist nations. In response to the initial move, Israel protested that it would serve only to increase tension in the Middle East. The real objection of Israel was succinctly expressed by the Israeli delegate to the UN. who charged that:

> ...the sponsors of the request for a special de-
> bate on Palestine were in effect backing
> another organization--the Palestine Liberation
> Organization-commited to the destruction of
> a member stated of the United Nations.[101]

But, the President of the Assembly, Abdelaziz Bouteflika of Algeria, disregarded Israel's protest and ruled that the request had been accepted without objection. As a result of this decision by the President of the Assembly, a separate full debate on the "Palestinian question" was placed on the agenda of the U.N. Assembly.

The suspicion of Israel that this move by Arab and African countries was a camouflage for a more serious affront to Israel proved to be accurate at the 1975 or thirtieth U.N. session. The next move against Israel by Arab nations and their African allies was a logical sequel to gaining a full debate on the "Palestinian question": recognition of the Palestine Liberation

Organization by the United Nations.

The Palestine Liberation Organization is the Arab
guerilla warfare organization which has as its goal the capture and
return to the Arab people of all territory seized and occupied
by Israel. This organization is seen by some African states
as equivalent in objective and operation to the African liberation movements in southern Africa. To have the United Nations
recognize the PLO as a legitimate representative of Arab
people and have it participate in all political deliberations
designed to resolve the Middle East Crisis would be like sanctioning or supporting the use of violence or military efforts
against Israel in the Middle East.

The draft resolution in the U.N. that called for the
recognition of the Palestine Liberation Organization was
prepared and submitted by 69 member countries. The non-
Arab backers of the resolution included the Soviet Union,
China, other communist countries and black African and non-
aligned countries. The resolution called for:

> The invitaion of the Palestine Liberation
> Organization, the representative of the
> Palestinian people to participate in all
> efforts, deliberations and conferences on
> the Middle East which are held under the
> auspices of the United Nations, on an equal
> footing with other parties....102

The proposed resolution giving recognition to the PLO
was adopted by a vote of 105 to 4 with 20 abstentions. The
vote distribution accurately reflects the countries which gave
support to the Arab-led effort to take militant action against
Israel. The four dissenting votes were cast by Bolivia, the
Dominican Republic, Israel and the United States. The countries abstaining on the resolution were: Britain, Belgium,
Denmark, Luxemburg, the Netherlands, West Germany, Austrlia
Burma, Canada, Iceland, and Latin American st tes. Only
three European countries, France, Ireland and Italy, voted in
favor of this resolution. The countries constituted an over-
whelming majority in favor of the resolution were the Arab,
African and communist states. Thus, African countries gave their
full suport to this move against Israel in the United Nations.

The militant political implications and significance of this move by Arab and African countries in the United Nations was succinctly expressed when an observer of the United Nations noted:

> In the 29 years of the United Nations, only representatives of member states have addressed the General Assembly so far. African Liberation movements were in past years permitted to expound their views at the United Nations headquarters but only in committee meetings.[103]

It was unprecendented to permit a liberation movement to participate in the U.N. General Assembly Debate with equal status of member nations. The extent of the recognition to be afforded the Palestine Liberation Organization in the U.N. was not only participation in full debate in the United Nations Assembly as called for in the resolution proposed by the Arab and African countries. This was augmented by a subsequent ruling by the President of the U.N. Assembly, on November 8, 1974, that the Palestinian representative who would participate in the debate on the "Question of Palestine" would be afforded the status of a delegation since the PLO had been invited by the General Assembly. The impact of his decision was to afford a non-governmental group the status and protocol of an officially accredited representative of member states of the United Nations.

Furthermore, the Arab-African states won support by the Assenbly to restrict Israel's participation in the U.N. debate on the "Palestine Question". The U.N. Assembly approved a proposal by Arab-African nations to limit each nation to one major speech in the debate on the issue of Palestine. . Israe expressed the view that this move was an attempt to "muzzle" Israel's right to speak. Such a restriction in the debate of the United Nations was unprecedented.

The momentum of militant/radical confrontation against Israel evinced during the twenty-ninth session was not to diminish or subside. At the thirteith or 1975 session, African nations

were calling for stronger radical action against Israel.
The chairman of the Organization of African Unity, President
Idi Amin of Uganda, addressed the United Nations in that capa-
city at the 1975 session. In his address condemning colonialism, neocolonialism, and Zionism, Amin "...called for
the expulsion of Israel from the United Nations and for the
extinction of Israel as a State'."[104]

While the specific actions called for by the chairman
of the O.A.U. were not adopted by the General Assembly, Africn
nations did play a decisive role in instituting certain actions
against Israel during the 1975 session. On November 10, 1975
the General Assembly adopted an Arab initiated resolution defining-
Zionisn as a 'form of racism and racial discrimination.'[205]
Thus, Israel was cast as comparable to the oppressive white-
minority racial and colonialist regimes of southern Africa.

Africa's role in this move was crucial. The anti-Zionism
draft resolution originating in the General Assembly's
Social, Humnitarian, and Cultural Committee, in which the vote
fell mainly on black African delegates. It took the form of an
amendment to a text condeming racism and colonialism.

Having been approved by the Social, Humanitarian and Cultural
Committee, the resolution was adopted by the U.N. body by a
vote of 72-35, with 32 abstentions. The majority was constituted
of the votes of Arab and other Islamic countries, communist
nations, Brazil, Mexico, and many third world countries in
Africa and Asia. While the support of African nations was very
significant, it was not unanimous. Four African countries
opposed the resolution: Central African Republic, Ivory Coast,
Liberia, Swaziland.

Variation Among African Nations On The Middle East Crisis

We turn now to the question of whether particular
geographic blocs had a predilection for the use of one particular type of technique of influence more than the others on
the Middle East Crisis. Table VIII shows the percentage of
nations within each bloc calling for each of the various techniques of influence in the U.N. Debate on the issue for each year
between 1967 and 1975. Table IX summarizes the date in Table
VIII, showing the overall percentage of the various techniques
of influence recommended by the geographical blocs for the whole

PERCENTAGE OF AFRICAN NATIONS WITHIN EACH BLOC WHICH FAVORED EACH TYPE OF RECOMMENDATION IN THE UNITED NATIONS ON THE ISSUE OF THE MIDDLE EAST CRISIS

TABLE—VIII

	PERSUASION									ISOLATION								
	'67	'68	'69	'70	'71	'72	'73	'74	'75	'67	'68	'69	'70	'71	'72	'73	'74	'75
CENTRAL AFRICA	50	50	50	33	50	33	33	0	17	0	0	0	0	0	0	33	0	17
EAST AFRICA	83	100	67	33	83	50	17	33	17	0	0	17	0	0	0	17	0	0
NORTH AFRICA	33	50	50	50	67	33	0	0	17	0	0	0	17	0	0	17	0	0
WEST AFRICA	56	47	41	41	71	71	12	47	21	0	0	0	0	0	0	6	0	0
SOUTHERN AFRICA (Black Majority Regimes)	67	50	0	0	25	25	0	25	25	0	0	0	0	0	0	0	0	0

TABLE – VIII CONTINUED

	MILITANT/RADICAL CONFRONTATION									NO RECOMMENDATION								
	'67	'68	'69	'70	'71	'72	'73	'74	'75	'67	'68	'69	'70	'71	'72	'73	'74	'75
CENTRAL AFRICA	0	0	0	0	0	0	0	17	0	50	50	50	67	50	67	33	83	67
EAST AFRICA	0	0	0	0	0	0	0	17	50	17	0	17	67	17	50	67	50	33
NORTH AFRICA	0	0	17	17	0	0	17	67	0	67	50	33	17	32	67	67	33	83
WEST AFRICA	0	0	0	0	0	0	0	0	0	44	53	59	59	29	29	88	53	79
SOUTHERN AFRICA (Black Majority Regimes)	0	0	0	0	0	0	25	0	0	33	50	100	100	75	75	75	75	75

111

PERCENTAGE OF AFRICAN NATIONS WITHIN EACH BLOC WHICH
FAVORED EACH TYPE OF RECOMMENDATION FROM 1967-1975
IN THE UNITED NATIONS ON THE ISSUE OF THE MID-EAST CRISIS

TABLE - IX

	PERSUASION	ISOLATION	MILITANT/ RADICAL CONFRONTATION	NO RE- COMMENDATION
CENTRAL AFRICA	36	6	2	58
EAST AFRICA	54	4	7	35
NORTH AFRICA	33	4	13	41
SOUTHERN AFRICA (Black Majority Regimes)	21	0	6	73
WEST AFRICA	43	7	0	55

112

period, 1967-1975. In both tables, the recommendations are
categorized as in previous chapters as: Persuasion, Isolation,
Militant/radical confrontation or No recommendation.

Table IX reveals that the most conciliatory bloc on the
Middle East Crisis was that of the East African states. This
is based on the fact that 54% of the nations within the East
African bloc called for the use of persuasion techniques of
influence from 1967-1975 in the U.N., while only 4% of the
nations within the bloc called for isolation, 7% called for
militant/radical confrontation techniques, and 35% of the nations
made no recommendation on the issue for the period.

The most militant bloc on the Middle East Crisis, according to Table IX, appears to have been the North African states
based on the fact that the highest percentage of nations within
any bloc calling for militant/radical confrontation techniques
from the period of 1967-1975 in the U.N. Debate was 13%.

The data also reveals that the most silent bloc on the issue
in the U.N. Debate(was the issue in the U.N. Debate)was the
southern African (Black majority Regimes). 73% of the nations
within this bloc made no recommendation on the issue from
1967-1975 in the U.N. Debate sessions. This consituted the
highest percentage of nations within any bloc to refrain from
making any recommendation of action.

Table IX further reveals that the most vociferous bloc
on the issue of the Middle East Crisis was the East African
States since 65% of the nations within the bloc made recommendations on the issue during the period from 1967-1975 in the
U.N. This constituted the highest percentage of nations within any bloc making recommendations of action on the issue.

The high degree of non-participation in the U.N. Debate
which is reflected on the "No-recommendation" category of
Table IX and Table VII needs explaining at this point. The
"No-recommendation" category in Table IX and Table VII represents
the percentage of nations that did not participate in the U.N.

113

General Debate on the issue of the Middle East Crisis
because they either made no speech or did not make a
specific recommendation of action to be taken on the
problem of the Middle East when they did make a speech.
The levels of non-participation of the various geographical
blocs (Table IX) and the overall positions of all African
nations (Table VII) approach the 50% or better level for the
vast majority of the U.N. sessions between 1967-1975. This
perhaps can be explained by the fact that many African nations
were still concerned about alienating Israel as an important
source of technical aid for economic development. While
committed to the Arab nations, they may have felt that a
safe strategy was to be silent with respect to specific recommendations for action on the Middle East Crisis.

79. Frank Gervasi, The Case For Israel, New York, 1967, pg. 24.

80. Ibid, Pg. 72.

81. Ibid.

82. Ibid., pg. 81.

83. Ibid.

84. Gervasi, pg. 85.

85. Malcolm Kerr, "The Middle East Conflict", Foreign Policy Association Headline Series, October 1968, No. 191, pg. 18.

86. Ibid.

87. U.N. Resolution 242 (XII)

88. Colin Legum, "Israel's Year on Africa: A Study of Secret Diplomacy, "Africa Contemporary Record, Vol. III (London, 1972), p.g. A125.

89. Ibid., p. A126

90. Ibid.

91. Ibid.

92. Ibid. p. A130

93. United Nations Document, A/PV. 2244, September 26, 1974.

94. United Nations Document, A/PV 2245, September 26, 1974.

95. New York Times, May 26, 1973, pg. 9.

96. New York Times, May 26, 1973, pg. 9.

97. Ibid.

98. Ibid.

99. Ibid.

100. United Nations Document, A/PV, 2296, November 22, 1974.

101. New York Times, September 22, 1974, p.1

102. United Nations Document, A/P.V. 2399, November 10, 1975.

103. New York Times, September 30, 1974. p.7

104. United Nations Document, A/PV. 2370, October 1, 1975.

105. United Document, A/PV. 2400, November 10, 1975.

CHAPTER V

ECONOMIC DEVELOPMENT AND AFRICAN NATIONS
IN THE UNITED NATIONS

The purpose of this chapter will be to examine how
African nations responded to the issue of economic development in the U.N. between the years 1967-1975. Economic
development was the third issue of greatest concern to
African nations in the U.N. during this period; 84% of all
African nations addressing the U.N. General Debate between 1967-1975 raised the issue before the world body.

As in previous chapters, we will proceed by (1) examining some relevant background material on foreign policy
actions by African nations relating to the issue of economic
development, (2) attempting to identify the various methods of
influence favored by African nations to gain compliance to
the relevant U.N. resolutions and principles on economic development, (3) determining the percentages of African nations
with respect to their preferred strategies of influence, (4)
determining variation by geographical blocs among African
nations on the issue of economic development. However, we
will show that this issue was unique as compared to the others
we have considered.

We will first give a more detailed explanation of the
issue of economic development, and outline the U.N. resolutions
and principles that have been established by the world body
on this problem.

"Economic development" was perceived by African nations to
relate to all underdeveloped nations of the world not only to
Africa. This perception was to have a decisive effect on the
strategies employed by African nations to influence the issue
in the United Nations. African nations defined "economic
development" generally as the need to strengthen and eventually
bring about self-sufficient, unexploited economies in the
developing nations and developed nations; the transfer of technology; and the transfer of capital to the developing nations
to finance economic development.

117

African nations, as well as the vast majority of the
nations of Latin America and Asia repeatedly expressed the
view that the international economic order has contributed
and presently contributes to the persistent stagnation of
economic growth of the Third World. This appears most
evident with regard to the system of international trade.
These nations contend that the international terms of trade
work to the detriment of their economic development. As
stated by the representative of Liberia in the General
Assembly in 1972:

> The devloping countries are continuing
> to experience a deteriation in terms of
> trade with world prices for their primary
> commodities falling steadily while those
> of the manufactured goods they import,
> including essential capital and consumer
> goods, are constantly rising. [104]

The problem of capital and technology was stated by the
representative of Dahomey:

> ...For its development the third world
> fundamentally needs capital as well as
> technical expertise, and the practical
> abilities necessary to use such exper-
> tise. The success of this development
> requires that the transfer of this
> capital and technology take place without
> overwhelming the recipient with exorbitant
> repayment schedules and without placing
> them in a situation that prevents them
> from controlling their own economic priorities
> and their own social structures. [105]

African nations also described the issue of "economic
development" in terms of the existing and growing d fferences
between the level of development of the economies of the
Third World and those of the developed nations. This view
is reflected in the observation by Ethiopia's representative,

typical of the African's nation assessment:

> . . . The gap between the developed and
> the developing nations is thus increasing
> rather than decreasing as has hopefully been
> anticipated with the launching of the Second
> development Decade. . . In view of this it
> therefore becomes incumbent upon all members
> of the international community to review their
> solemn commitments to the struggle against the
> basic economic and social ills impeding the
> achievement of an improved quality of life for
> all mankind.[106]

The United Nations And Economic Development

The problem of underdevelopment as perceived by African
and Third World nations did not receive significant attention
from the U.N. until the late 1950's. Upon its inception, the
Organization's immediate concern with economic problems was
the reconstruction of war-torn Europe. The specific issue of
economic problems of developing countries was not an issue of
grave concern during the early years of the Organization because the number of Third World countries represented in the
body was very small.

The United Nations Charter provided for an organ which
was to address itself to and consider economic, social, and
related problems: the Economic and Social Council (ECOSOC).
The functions and power of ECOSOC have been described by
Herman Finer as the following:

> ...(a) It is empowered (Article 66, paragraph 1)
> to carry out, within the scope of its competence.
> general recommendations of the General Assembly.
> (b) it has the power (article 62, paragraphs
> 1, 1 and 4)to make recommendations on its own
> initiative with respect to international economic
> social, and other humanitarian matters, and pre-
> pare draft conventions for submission to the
> General Assembly and to call international con-

ferences. (c) another responsibility (article 64) is to obtain regular reports from the economic, social, and specialized organizations and agencies brought into relationship with the Organization...(d) it may communicate its observations in these reports to the General Assembly. (e) it may furnish information to the Security Council and must assist the Security Council upon its request. (f) it may, with the approval of the General Assembly, perform services at the request of members of the United Nations and at the request of specialized agencies.[107]

Thus, ECOSOC had a broad range of functions including initiating studies and reports, making reports and recommendations to the General Assembly, the Security Council, members of the U.N. and specialized agencies as well as implementing recommendations and performing various services on issues related to economic, social, cultural and educational matters. ECOSOC has attempted to carry out its functions in part by creating Regional Economic Commissions for Europe, Asia and the Pacific (formerly Asia and the Far East), Western Asia, Latin America, and Africa.

The United Nations efforts to address itself to the issue of economic development began with the establishment of the Special Fund. On October 14, 1958, the General Assembly adopted Resolution 1240 (XIII) which created the Special Fund whose purpose was summarized by Gerard G. Mangone as follows: "The Special fund was designed to undertake pre-investment surveys of natural resources, with investigations of the feasibility of exploiting such resources to achieve national development goals, and to establish or strengthen technical training as well as educational and applied research that might hasten economic and social progress."[108] The Special Fund was to concentrate on relatively large projects as opposed to many small projects; it was essentially a pre-investment development assistance agency and not a capital development fund.

A move toward establishing a means of giving capital
for the purpose of economic development began in the General
Assembly in 1960. However, the idea of creating a United
Nations Capital Development Fund was adopted by the General
Assembly only "in principle" at the fifteenth or 1960 session.
A committee to consider all prepratory measures was established. It was not until 1966, however, six years after the Geneal
Assembly created "in principle" a capital development fund,
that the body actually created one. The purpose of the fund
was "to assist developing countries in the development of
their economies by supplementing existing sources of capital
assistance by means of grants and loans, particularly long,
term loans made free of interest or at low interest rates.'[109]
Resolution 2186 (Xx) of the General Assembly created the
Capital Development Fund on December 13, 1966 and provided
for a pledging conference for the fall of 1967. The pledging
conference was boycotted by all the Western nations except
Netherlands and all eastern European nations, except Yuog-
slavia,[110] because they opposed the resolution. Thus, the
Capital Development Fund was a failure.

At the sixteenth United Nations session, The General
Assembly enacted, through Resolution 1710 (XVI) on December
19, 1961, the first United Nations Development Decade. The
First Development Decade designated the decade of the 60's
as a decade in which member nations and internal institutions
were to intensify their efforts to bring about sustained
economic growth in developing nations. The United Nations
Development Decade set as a target for the end of the Decade
a minimum annual rate of growth of aggregate national income
of five percent for developing nations. The resolution es-'
tablished the Deveopment Decade called for the achievement of
this goal through intensification of international economic cooperation between developed nations, the developing nations
and international institutions.

A special body was established by the U.N. to consider
and address itself exclusively to the issue. The United
Conference on Trade and Development (UNCTAD) was created by

the United Nations to promote international trade, particularly with the aim to accelerate economic development.
The first conference was to meet in 1964 in Geneva. The
conference was to convene every four years subsequent to
the 1964 meeting.

At the twentieth United Nations session (1965) the General
Assembly established the U.N. Development Programme.[111]
The Development Programme was simply the merger of the Special
Fund and a program of ECOSOC, the Expanded Technical Assis-
tance Program.* The merger of these technical assistance pro-
grams was aimed at improving the administration of United
Nations' assistance to the developing nations.

The following year, the United Nations established the
Industrial Development Organization, through Resolution 2151
(XXI), November 17, 1966. The objective of this organization
was "...to promote industrial development, in accordance
with Article I, Paragraph 3, and Article 55 and 56 of the
Charter of the United Nations, and by encouraging the mobilization
of national and international resources to assist in, promote
and accelerate the industrilization of the developing countries,
with particular emphasis on the manufacturing sector."[112]

The Industrial Development Organization was to provide assistance through research programs, studies and recommendations for
industrialization in individual developing countries.

In 1970, the General Assembly adopted a resolution establishing the Second Development Decade. Resolution 2626
(XXV) called for the developed countries to contribute
Financial aid for economic development to developing nations
amounting to one percent of their GNP. The Second Development
Decade called for the developing nations to achieve a growth
rate of six percent annually by the end of the decade.

Strategies of Influence On Economic Development

In seeking to gain compliance for U.N. resolutions
relating to the issue of economic development, African
nations in the United Nations recommended exclusively techniques of persuasion between 1967-1975. This shown by the data
contained in Table X and Table XI.

Table X shows all the various techniques of influence
called for or recommended by all African nations in their
U.N. General Debate speeches between 1967-1975. Here it is
clear that the only technique of infleunce recommended by
African nations on the issue of economic development was
persuasion. These data and all other data in this chapter
are drawn from Appendix III in which we provide a detailed
presentation of each African nation's broad policy position
and recommendation of action on the issue of economic development.
The Appendix indicates whether a nation made a speech in debate,
whether it discussed the issue of economic development, the
broad policy position taken on the issue, and the specific
recommendation of action or influence on the issue.

Table XI summarizes the data in Table X by showing the
percentage of African nations in the U.N. favoring the use of
the various techniques of influence on the issue of economic
development for all the years between 1967-1975. Table XI
shows that a significant proportion of African nations tended
to make no recommendation for action or infleunce technique
on the issue of economic development in U.N. General Debate.
In fact, the average percentage of African nations refraining
from making recommendations on the issue during the nine U.N.
sessions between 1967-1975 was 42%.

The table also shows that African nations favored only the
use of persuasion techniques of influence on the issue of economic development. There was no recommendation for either
isolation techniques or militant/radical confrontation on this
issue at any session of the U.N. General Debate from 1967-1975.
The average percentage of African nations recommending persuasion on the issue of economic development between 1967-1975
in the U. N. General Debate was 58%.

INFLUENCE TECHNIQUES FAVORED BY AFRICAN NATIONS IN THE UNITED NATIONS
ON THE ISSUE OF ECONOMIC DEVELOPMENT
TABLE – X

	'67	'68	'69	'70	'71	'72	'73	'74	'75
Algeria	P	NS	P	P	P	NR	P	P	NR
Botswana	P	P	NR	NS	NS	NS	NS	P	NS
Burundi	P	P	P	NS	NS	P	P	P	NS
Cameroon	P	NR	NS	ND	P	P	NS	P	P
Central African Republic	NS	NS	P	NS	P	P	ND	P	NS
Chad	NR	NS	P	NS	P	P	NS	P	P
Congo (Brazzaville)	P	NS	P	P	P	P	P	P	P
Dahomey	NS	NS	NS	NS	P	P	P	P	P
Democratic Republic of Sao Tome & Principe	-	-	-	-	-	-	-	-	NS
Ethiopia	P	P	P	NS	P	NR	P	P	NS
Equatorial Guinea	-	NS	ND	NS	NS	NS	P	P	P
Gabon	P	P	NS	NS	P	NR	NR	P	P
Gambia	P	NS	NS	NS	NS	P	NS	P	NS
Ghana	P	P	NS	P	P	P	P	P	P

Key --   I=Isolation   - = Non-Member of U.N.   ND=No Discussion   NR=No Recommendation
NS=No Speech   P=Persuasion   MRC=Militant Radical Confrontation

124

TABLE-X CONTINUED

	'67	'68	'69	'70	'71	'72	'73	'74	'75
Guinea	NO	P	P	P	P	P	P	P	NS
Ivory Coast	NS	NS	P	NS	P	P	NS	P	NS
Kenya	ND	P	P	P	P	P	ND	P	P
Lesotho	P	P	NS	NS	NS	NS	P	P	P
Liberia	P	P	P	P	P	P	P	P	P
Libya	P	NR	ND	NR	ND	ND	ND	P	ND
Madagascar	NR	P	NS	ND	P	NR	P	NS	P
Malawi	NR	ND	NS	NS	NS	ND	NS	NS	NS
Mali	ND	NS	P	NS	NS	NR	P	P	P
Mauritania	ND	NS	P	NS	P	NR	P	P	P
Morocco	P	P	P	ND	P	ND	ND	P	P
Niger	P	NS	NS	NS	P	P	ND	ND	NS
Nigeria	P	P	P	NS	P	P	P	P	P
Peoples' Republic of Mozambique	–	–	–	–	–	–	–	–	P

TABLE-X CONTINUED

	'67	'68	'69	'70	'71	'72	'73	'74	'75
Republic of Cape Verde	-	-	-	-	-	-	-	-	NS
Rwanda	P	P	P	P	P	P	P	P	P
Senegal	ND	P	P	NS	NR	P	P	P	P
Sierra Leone	NR	ND	P	P	P	P	P	P	P
Somalia	ND	P	ND	ND	NR	P	ND	NS	P
Sudan	P	P	NR	ND	NR	P	P	NS	ND
Swaziland	-	NS	NR	NS	NS	P	NS	P	NS
Togo	P	P	NS	P	P	P	NS	P	P
Tunisia	P	P	P	P	P	ND	ND	P	P
Uganda	P	P	P	NS	P	ND	NS	P	P
United Arab Republic	ND	ND	NR	NS	ND	P	ND	ND	NS
United Republic of Tanzania	P	P	P	NS	P	P	P	P	P
Upper Volta	P	NS	P	NS	P	NR	P	P	P
Zaire	P	P	P	NS	NS	P	P	P	P
Zambia	NR	NR	P	P	P	P	P	P	P

PERCENTAGE BREAKDOWN OF VARIOUS ACTIONS RECOMMENDED BY AFRICAN NATIONS ON THE ISSUE OF ECONOMIC DEVELOPMENT IN THE UNITED NATIONS

TABLE-XI

		1967	1968	1969	1970	1971	1972	1973	1974	1975
PERSUASION	Negotiation	0	0	0	0	5	0	0	5	18
	Appeal	60	57	50	27	62	62	56	80	42
	Total	60	57	50	27	67	62	56	85	60
ISOLATION		0	0	0	0	0	0	0	0	0
MILITANT/RADICAL CONFRONTATION	Support Armed Struggle	0	0	0	0	0	0	0	0	0
	Expulsion From United Nations	0	0	0	0	0	0	0	0	0
	Total	0	0	0	0	0	0	0	0	0
NO ACTION RECOMMENDED		40	43	50	73	33	38	44	15	40

The use of persuasion by African nations was also
marked by a high degree of cooperation with other Third
World Countries on this issue. African nations joined Asian
and Latin American countries to form the "Group of 77"
at the conclusion of the first session of the United Conference on Trade and Development in 1964. The Group of 77,
which later expanded to over one hundred developing countries
of the world, united "...to pursue their joint efforts towards
economic and social development, peace and prosperity."[113]
The Group of 77 scheduled itself to convene prior to each
UNCTAD session "...in order to harmonize the positions of
developing countries and to formulate joint programmes of
action in all matters related to trade and development."[114]

The Group of 77 adopted the Charter of Algiers in 1967
on the eve of the Second United Nations Conference on Trade
and Development scheduled to be held in 1968. The Charter
of Algiers, while outlining a number of specific trade and
development policies and a programme of action it would have
liked to see UNCTAD adopt, also outlined future activities
of the Group of 77. They were to " meet at the ministerial
level as often as this may be deemed necessary, and always
prior to the convening of sessions of the United Nations
Conference on Trade and development in order to harmonize
the positions of developing countries and to formulate joint
programmes of action in all matters related to trade and development."[115] The second important activity of the
Group of 77 was to be six-high-level goodwill missions "..to
visit capitals of developed and socialist countries composed
of at least one, and if possible two special envoys accredited
by Heads of States from each of the three regional groups
within the Group of 77."[116] These goodwill missions were to
be completed before the end of November 1967. The purpose
of the goodwill missions were made quite clear by the
Charter of Algiers:

> These missions, entrusted with the task
> of informing and persuading, shall acquaint
> the respective Governments of the countries
> to be visited of the conclusion of the
> meeting,so as to contribute to the creation

128

of the best possible conditions for
negotiations on the programme of action
at the second session of the conference.[117]

Finally, the Charter of Algiers called upon the President of
the Ministerial Meeting of the Group of 77 to present the
document to the General Assembly of the United Nations.

The outcome of the Second United Nations Conference on
Trade and Development was assessed as unsatisfactory by African
and other third world nations. The session was held in
New Delhi in 1968. Dissatisfaction with the outcome was
expressed by many African nations. The observation of Gabon
is representative of the response of African nations to the
Second UNCTAD:

> The results of this conference
> well, known showed that those to whom
> the charter was addressed were not pre-
> pared to appreciate its scope and to
> grant it their immediate support in
> order to bring about that moral solidarity
> between rich and poor countries which is
> needed if the desired balance in world
> development is to be achieved.[118]

The Group of 77 next placed hopes in the Third Conference
on Trade and Development which was to be held in Santiago,
Chile in 1972. Prior to the Third UNCTAD, the Group of 77
convened in Lima, Peru from October 25, to November 7, 1971
to harmonize their positions on development issues. This
meeting produced what is known as the Lima Declaration. The
Lima Declaration was a document of principles and a program
of action outlined by ninety-six developing countries for
accelerating the development process.

The Lima Declaration also included a section which defined future activities of the Group of 77. For effective
participation at the third session of the UNCTAD, the Group
of 77 declared that it:

> 1. ...is firmly and unequivocally resolved

> the developing countries to
> determine what their economic and
> trade relations with the developed
> countries should be. . .[120]

The only decision which the third UNCTAD made that African
and other Third World countries considered positive was the
selection of the 25 least developed nations for preferential
and special aid.

The next attempt by African and Third World nations to
influence the issue of "economic development" occured in
1974. The Third World countries petitioned for the convening of a Special United Nations Session which would address
itself exclusively to the problem of "raw materials and economic development". This move was led by Algeria in an
attempt to correct the imbalance of economic development
between the industrialized nations and the 96 underdeveloped
nations.

Algeria successfully won the support of the 68 nations
necessary to have the U.N. Assembly convene in special session.
The Special Session was historic in that it was the sixth ever
to be held by the United Nations and it was the first ever
devoted to economic matters. Other special sessions of the
U.N. have dealt with Palestine, South-West Africa, and
Peace-keeping.

The Sixth Special Session of the U.N. was convened from
April-May, 1974. At the historic session, the Third World
countries offered debate on a Declaration on the Establishment
of a new International Order, which was adopted by the United
Nations. The Declaration essentially called for bridging
the gap between the developed countries and the developing
countries by increasing the cooperation of the international
community. This general objective was to be realized by all
nations embracing and giving full respect to the principles of
sovereignty of every state over its natural resources, resti-
tution and compensation to colonial territories for the exploitation of their natural resources while under colonial
domination, the regulation of activities of transitional
corporation, equitable prices for raw materials and manufactured

to maintain and further strengthen the
unity and solidarity of the Group, and
so to organize themselves as to be able
to ensure the maximum impact and effect
at the third session of the United Nations
Conference on Trade and Development.'

2.   To achieve this desired impact, the Group
has decided to appoint a working party
in Geneva which will prepare the required
documentation and draft resolutions and
coordinate the appropriate activities of
the members of the Group as they bear on
the goals to be achieved at the Conference.
Accordingly, the membership of the working
party will be be kept openedended so that
any member of the Group or // may have un-
impeded access to its deliberations without
affecting its efficient functioning. 119

The response of African nations to the third session of
UNCTAD was, as before, that of disappointment. The observation
by Nigeria was typical:

The reluctance of the developed countries
to meet the minimum requirements of the
developing countries, as set out in the
Declaration adopted at the Second Ministerial Meeting of the Group of 77 developing
countries in Lima 1971, was clearly shown on
almost every problem discussed at the session.
In the face of this apathy on the part of the
advanced countries towards taking the basic step
in the implementation of a Strategy which was
carefully and elaborately worked out, can we
in the Third World continue to entrust our
Economic fortunes to others? It is the view of
Nigeria that this situation calls for closer
cooperation and deeper consultations among

131

products in international trade. Preferential and non-reciprocal treatment for developing countries in all areas of international economic cooperation, favorable conditions for the transfer of financial resources and technology to developing countries for development. The Special Session of the United Nations was the culmination of attempts by African nations in collaboration with other Third World countries to influence the issue of economic development during the period of focus of our study. Now, let's examine the nature of variation among African nations on the issue of economic development.

Variation Among African Nations on Economic Development

We found no significant variation among African nations on the issue of economic development with respect to the strategy of influence favored from 1967-1975.

Table XII compares the percentage of nations in each bloc which expressed favor for the various techniques of influence for each U.N. session between 1967-1975. This table shows that there was never a preference expressed by any bloc of African nations for the use of techniques of either isolation or militant/radical confrontation on the issue of economic development.

Table XIII summarizes the data in Table XII by showing the percentage of nations within each geographical bloc that recommended the various types of action of influence on the issue of economic development over the nine year period between 1967-1975. This table enables us to determine which geographical bloc tended to be the most, militant, concil-iatory, vociferous and silent on the issue of economic development based on their recommendations of the various actions of influence.

As the data shows, no bloc was militant on the issue in terms of recommending the use of militant/radical confrontation techniques of influence. All African blocs were conciliatory in the issue of economic development; persuasion was the only technique of influence recommended throughout

132

PERCENTAGE OF AFRICAN NATIONS WITHIN EACH BLOC WHICH FAVORED EACH TYPE OF RECOMMENDATION IN THE UNITED NATIONS ON THE ISSUE OF ECONOMIC DEVELOPMENT

TABLE – XII

GEOGRAPHICAL BLOC	PERSUASION									ISOLATION								
	'67	'68	'69	'70	'71	'72	'73	'74	'75	'67	'68	'69	'70	'71	'72	'73	'74	'75
CENTRAL AFRICA	83	67	83	33	50	100	83	83	50	0	0	0	0	0	0	0	0	0
EAST AFRICA	50	83	83	33	83	67	50	83	83	0	0	0	0	0	0	0	0	0
NORTH AFRICA	67	33	67	33	67	17	33	83	50	0	0	0	0	0	0	0	0	0
WEST AFRICA	50	35	65	24	77	77	65	83	63	0	0	0	0	0	0	0	0	0
SOUTHERN AFRICA	67	50	0	0	0	25	25	75	25	0	0	0	0	0	0	0	0	0

TABLE – XII CONTINUED

GEOGRAPHICAL BLOC	MILITANT RADICAL									NO RECOMMENDATION								
	'67	'68	'69	'70	'71	'72	'73	'74	'75	'67	'68	'69	'70	'71	'72	'73	'74	'75
CENTRAL AFRICA	0	0	0	0	0	0	0	0	0	17	33	17	67	50	0	17	17	50
EAST AFRICA	0	0	0	0	0	0	0	0	0	50	17	17	67	17	33	50	17	17
NORTH AFRICA	0	0	0	0	0	0	0	0	0	33	67	33	67	33	83	67	17	50
WEST AFRICA	0	0	0	0	0	0	0	0	0	50	65	35	76	23	23	35	17	37
SOUTHERN AFRICA	0	0	0	0	0	0	0	0	0	33	50	100	100	100	75	75	25	75

Percentages do not always total 100 because of rounding off.

PERCENTAGE OF AFRICAN NATIONS WITHIN EACH BLOC WHICH
FAVORED EACH TYPE OF RECOMMENDATION FROM 1967–1975
IN THE UNITED NATIONS ON THE ISSUE OF ECONOMIC DEVELOPMENT

TABLE – XIII

GEOGRAPHICAL BLOC	PERSUASION	ISOLATION	MILITANT / RADICAL CONFRONTATION	NO RE- COMMENDATION
CENTRAL AFRICA	70	0	0	30
EAST AFRICA	59	0	0	41
NORTH AFRICA	50	0	0	50
SOUTHERN AFRICA (Black Regimes)	30	0	0	70
WEST AFRICA	61	0	0	39

the period.

The most silent bloc on the issue appears to have been
the Southern Africa (Black Regimes), since 70% of all their
U.N. recommendation between 1967-1975 consisted of no
specific call of action. In contrast, the most vociferous
bloc on the issue appears to be the Central African bloc
of states being that only for 30% of their recommendations
between 1967-1975 consisted of no call for any type of
action. This was the lowest percent for no recommendations
for any bloc.

Variation although not existing in the explicit preference
for various types of action or influence on the issue of
economic development, existed in terms of simply those nations
who tended to make no recommendation of action on the issue,
cumulative 42% and some variation in specific recommendations
of persuasion, e.g., between "negotiation and appeal".
Along geographical bloc , variation took the same form with
variation simply existing among the nations within each bloc
either favoring "persuasion" techniques or no recommendation
of action being made.

These variations are less significant than the wider
variations on other issues, and on this issue there were
no recommendations for techniques of isolation or militant/
radical confrontation.

In order to understand the techniques favored by African
nations to exert influence on the issue of "economic development"
we should notice a significant difference between this and
other issues of concern to African nations in the United
Nations. That is, that it does not involve the violation of
some political principle that has been sanctioned by the U.N.
or international community. Decolonization deals with a
violation of the political principle of "self-determination"
which had been recognized by the international community
through the United Nations and other international organizations.
Likewise, the Middle East Crisis was seen by African nations
to involve the violation of the political principle of
"territorial integrity".

Some explanation is needed for the unusual situation where only one type of influence was recommended and used, namely persuasion. The explanation may rest on the fact that economic development as an issue involves the voluntary transfer of resources from one society to another. There is no high standing clear principle in the United Nations, sanctioned by the world community that compels a nation to give its resources to another country. Economic development is not a political issue of the same type as decolonization or the Middle East Crisis. Persuasion becomes the only applicable technique of influence, since it would be difficult to use isolation or militant/radical confrontation against nations reluctant to give money and resources to another country. It would be hard to win the support of the international community in such a case.

137

104. United Nations Document, A/PV. 2051, October 3, 1972

105. United Nations Document, A/PV. 2061, October 10, 1972.

106. United Nations Document, A/PV. 2127. September 25, 1973.

107. Herman Finer, The United Nations Economic And Social Council (Boston, 1946), p.62.

108. Gerard J. Mangone, U.N. Administration of Economic And Social Program (New York, 1966), p. 178.

109. United Nations Document A/PV. 1492, December, 1966.

110. David Kay, New Nations in The United Nations, (New York 1970), p. 109.

111. Created by Resolution 2029 (XX) of the General Assembly on November 22, 1965.

112. United Nations Document, A/PV. 1468, November 17, 1946.

113. United Nations, Proceedings of the U.N. Conference on Trade and Development, Second Session, Vol. I, Report and Annexes, p. 431, 1968.

114. Ibid.

115. Ibid. Vol. I., Report and Annexes, p. 431, 1968.

116. Ibid.

117. Ibid.

118. United Nations Document, A/PV. 1677, October 2, 1968.

119. U.N. Proceedings, p. 405.

120. United Document, A/PV, 2048, October 2, 1972.

CHAPTER VI: CONCLUSION

In our study we have sought to examine some aspects of African nations' attempts to gain compliance with United Nations' resolutions on the issues of greatest concern to them in the period 1967-1975. We defined African nations as all independent black majority regimes on the continent of Africa.

Our first problem was to identify what issues in the United Nations were of the greatest concern to African nations. On the basis of content analysis of all the General Debate speeches by African nations in the United Nations between 1967-1975, we concluded that the issues of greatest concern to African nations were: decolonization, Middle East crisis, and economic development. These three issues were raised most frequently, among all issues we identified in Chapter II. Decolonization was raised by 94% of all African nations speaking in the U.N. Debate between 1967-1975; the Middle East Crisis was raised 90%, economic development, the third most important issue of concern, was raised by 81%.

When compared with earlier works which focused on identifying the issue of greatest concern prior to 1967, for instance in David Kay's work, New Nations in the United Nations, we have found that the issues of concern to Africa were essentially the same except one, namely, the emergence of the Middle East Crisis as an issue of key importance to African nation's as a result of increased pressure exerted by the North African states in the OAU following the 1967 war.

Content analysis of the speeches on each issue allowed us to identify various techniques of strategies expressed and favored by African nations on the issues of decolonization, Middle East Crisis, and economic development. The major categories are: (1) persuasion, (2) Isolation, and (3) militant/radical confrontation. On each issue we also sought to determine the degree of cohesion and the degree of geographic variation among African nations as to the use of these techniques.

The two basic hypotheses of our study were:

(1) African nations in the United Nations show discernible consistent patterns or strategies in their recommendations of techniques for gaining compliance to those United Nations resolutions and principles that relate to the issues of greatest concern to them.

(2) There exists variation among groups of African nations which tend to prefer the use of one particular strategy of influence more than another on various issues in gaining compliance to United Nations' principles and resolutions.

Our data does not confirm general cohesion among African nations in the U.N. General Debates on the use of the three types of influence. In fact our data reveals that a very significant proporation of African nations refrained from making recommendations of influence on the issues of decolo-nization, Middle East Crisis, and Economic Development (SEE table XIV). In other words one of our significant findings is that there existed a high degree of non- participation (both non-speaking and non-recommendation) in the U.N. debate on the part of many African nations. The overall percentages of African nations refraining from making recommendations of influence on the issue of decolonization over the nine year period between 1967-1975 was 49%. The average percentage of African nations refraining from making any specific recommen-dations on the issue of the Middle East Crisis between 1967-1975 was 53%. The average percentage of African nations failing to make specific recommendations of action or influence on the issue of economic development was 45%. Overall, 49% of African nations over the period of 1967-1975 remained silent as to recommendations of action on the issues of greatest concern to them. Clearly therefore, no general consensus or cohesion can be shown among African nations with respect to the differing strategies of influence on these issues.

140

Table XIV

OVERALL PERCENTAGE OF AFRICAN NATIONS FAVORING THE
VARIOUS STRATEGIES OF INFLUENCE ON THE THREE ISSUES
OF GREATEST CONCERN

	P	I	MRC	NR
Decolonization	23	9	19	49
Middle East	41	2	4	53
Economic Development	56	0	0	45

Key for various strategies of Influence: P=Persua-
sion, I=Isolation, MRC=Militant radical confrontation, NR=No Recommendation

141

However, those African nations which did make specific recommendations of strategies on the three various issues of concern tended to favor persuasive techniques of influence. Isolation appears to be the least favored strategy of influence.among African nations. Moreover, a considerable degree of consensus or cohesion was achieved on the issue of economic development, in that the African nations which did make recommendations favored only the use of "persuasion" techniques. The average percentage of African nations calling for persuasion techniques on the issue of economic development between 1967-1975 in the U.N. General Debaste was 56%.

On the issue of decolonization and the Middle East Crisis, African nations did not achieve a consensus or cohesion but merely a plurality of support for some techniques among those African nations which did make recommendations. On the issue of decolonization, the techniques of persuasion maintained a plurality of support in the period 1967-1971, while techniques of militant/radical confrontation received the plurality in the years 1972-1975. Isolation as a technique of influence on this issue did not receive any significant support. On the issue of the Middle East Crisis, African nations maintanined a plurality of support for the use of persuasion techniques of influence between 1967-1975 except for the year 1973. In 1973 those African nations that did make recommendations on the issue were evenly divided between persuasion and isolation techniques of influence.

In summary, it appears from the speeches of African nation: in the U.N. General Debate that most of those who were vociferous favored the use of persuasion on all issues throughout most or all of the period of this study, but on the issue of primary concern, decolonization, the preference shifted to militant/radical confrontation in the years 1972-1975.

With respect to geographic variation, our study reveals that on all three issue, decolonization, Middle,East Crisis and Economic development, the most silent in terms of making

142

the fewest recommendations during the U.N. sessions between 1967-1975, was the Southern Africa bloc (Black majority regimes). The most vociferous bloc, making the most recommendations on decolonization and the Middle East Crisis, was the East African states. The most vociferous bloc on the issue of economic development, was the Central African states.

The blocs vary in militancy according to the three issues. The F st African states were the most militant on the issue of decolonization, recommending the use of militant/radical techniques of influence more often between 1967-1975 in the U.N. General Debate than any other bloc. The most militant bloc on the issue of the Middle East was the North African states. No bloc was militant on the issue of economic development.

As Table XV shows the most conciliatory blocs on the various issues differed as well. The most conciliatory states on decolonization were the Central African states, in that more of these states (33%) called for the use of persuasion than in any other bloc on the issue. The most conciliatory on the issue of economic development.

Our study shows that "influence" as a process of attempting to gain compliance to U.N. resolutions and principles involves the use by African nations in the United Nation of three basic strategies, "persuasion", "isolation", and "militant/radical confrontation". Although African nations are not necessarily and clearly cohesive in the use of these techniques on issues of concern to them in the United Nations they, however, are the general strategies favored.

Another significant finding of our study relates to the question of cohesion of African nations in the U.N. While earlier studies on cohesion of African nations in the U.N. tend to maintain the thesis that African nations are very cohesive

PERCENTAGE OF NATIONS WITHIN EACH AFRICAN GEOGRAPHICAL BLOC FAVORING THE VARIOUS
STRATEGIES OF INFLUENCE ON THE THREE ISSUES OF GREATEST CONCERN IN THE U.N.

TABLE XV

GEOGRAPHICAL BLOC	PERSUASION			ISOLATION			MILITANT RADICAL CONFRONTATION		
	D	ME	ED	D	ME	ED	D	ME	ED
Central Africa	33	36	70	6	6	0	17	2	0
East Africa	24	54	59	22	4	0	32	7	0
North Africa	17	33	50	7	4	0	17	13	0
Southern Africa (black majority regime)	19	21	30	3	0	0	6	6	0
West Africa	22	43	61	11	7	0	19	0	0

Key: D=Decolonization ME=Middle East Crisis ED=Economic Development

as measured by their voting patterns in the U.N. our study enables us to make a more refined analysis of this issue.

That African nations are cohesive in the U.N. is not questioned in support of U.N. principles and resolutions. However, our data reveals that African nations lack cohesion in terms of strategies for gaining compliance.

In terms of foreign policy actions, our study shows that African nations are not cohesive in the international political system on the issues of concern in the U.N. In fact constant discrepancy persists between OAU commitment to militancy on issues, particularly decolonization, and continued support for persuasion by some African nations in the U.N. While most African nations frequently supported OAU policy declarations of militant stands against white-minority regimes, several of these same nations would disavow that position by engaging in persuasive methods in violations of principles of the OAU.

With respect to differences or popularity of various strategies according to issues, our data shows that persuasion (see Table XV) is the most favored on the decolonization issue among the various blocs, and militant radical confrontation ranked highest among the various blocs on the issue of decolonization. It is clear by this table that even among the various blocs isolation and militant/radical confrontation were not highly favored on the issues of the Middle East Crisis and economic development.

BIBLIOGRAPHY

BOOKS

Akpan. Moses E. African Goals and Diplomatic Strategies In The United Nations. North Quincy, Massachusetts: Christopher Publishing House, 1976.

Chamberlain, Waldo and Hovet, Thomas. A Chronology and Fact Book Of The United Nations, 1941-1976. Dobbs Ferry, New York: Oceana Publications, 1976.

El-Ayoutv, Yassin and Brooks, Hugh C. Africa and International Organization. Hague, Netherlands: Martinus Nijhoff, 1974

Emerson, Rupert and Padelford, Norman J. (eds). Africa and World Order. New York: Praeger Publishers, 1963

Finer, Herman. The United Nations Economic and Social Council. Boston: World Peace Foundation, 1946

Gervasi, Frank. The Case For Israel. New York: Viking Press, 1967.

Goodspeed, Stephen. The Nature And Function of International Organization. New York: Oxford University Press, 1959.

Hovet, Thomas. Africa In The United Nations. Chicago: North-Western University Press, 1963.

_____. Bloc Politics In The United Nations. Cambridge: Harvard University Press, 1960.

Ingham, Kenneth (ed). Foreign Relations of African States. London: Colston Research Society, 1974

Kay, David. New Nations In The United Nations. New York: Columbia University Press, 1970.

Ledow, Richard N. and Henderson, Gregory (eds). Divided Nations In A Divided World. New York: D. McKay Co., 1974.

Legum, Colin, Africa Contemporary Record. London: African Research Ltd., 1970.

_____. Pan-Africanism, A Short Political Guide. New
York: Praeger Publishers, 1965.

_____. South Africa: Crisis For The West. New York:
Praeger Publishers, 1964.

_____. (ed). The First U.N. Development Decade And
Its Lessons For The 1970's New York: Praeger Publishers,
1970.

_____. The United Nations And Southern Africa. New
York: African Publishing Company, 1970.

London Times (Insight Team). The Yom Kippur War. Garden City
New York: Doubleday & Company, 1974.

McKay Vernon. Africa In World Politics. Westport, Conneticut:
Greenwood Press, 1963.

Mangone, Gerard J. (ed). U.N. Administration of Economic And
Social Progress. New York: Columbia University Press,
1966.

Norris, John. An Examination Of The Sanction That Have Been
Imposed On The Republic Of South Africa And Rhodesia.
Urbana, Illinois: Thesis, University of Illinois, 1973.

Sharp, Walter R. The United Nations Economic And Social Council.
New York: Columbia University Press, 1969.

Sicherman, Harvey. The Yom Kippur War: End of Illusion?
Beverly Hills: Sage Publication, 1976.

Stoessinger, John G. The United Nations And The Superpowers.
New York: Random House, 1965.

Articles

"Africa At The U.N. - Thoughts On Emergent Continent", Africa
Today, October, 1960.

"Africa's Role in United Nations", Africa World, April 1960

"Africans At The United Nations", West Africa, October 1,
1960, No. 2261 p. 1125

"Afro-Asia Asserts Itself", West Africa, September 24, 1960. No. 2202, p. 5931.

"Agenda For Africa", West Africa, August 15, 1959, No. 2201, p. 593.

Arden-Clarke, Charles, "South West Africa, The Union, And The United Nations", African Affairs, January, 1960, Vol. 59, No. 234, p. 26-35.

Brecher, Micheal, "A Framework For Research On Foreign Policy Behavior", Journal of Conflict Resolution, March, 1969, Vol. 13, No. 1 pg. 75-102.

_____. "International Relations And Asian Studies: The Subordinate State System Of Southern Asia", World Politics, January 1963, Vol. 15, No. 2, p. 213-236.

Cohen, Sir Andrew, "The New Africa And The United Nations In Legum, Colin, Africa: A Handbook to the Continent. New York, Praeger Press, 1962.

Cottrell, W.F., "The U.N. and Africa", Annals Of The American Academy Of Political And Social Sciences, July, 1956, Vol. 306, pg. 55-61.

Gilelspie, Joan, "Africa's Voice At The United Nations", Africa Special Report, June, 1959, Vol. 4, No. 6, Pg. 13-14.

Jack, Homes A., "The 'African Assembly'," Africa Today, November, 1960, Vol. 7, No. 7, pg. 9-11, 14.

Kay, David, "The Impact of African States On The United Nations", International Organization, 1969, Vol. 23, No. 1,pg.20-48

Keith, Irvine, "African Nationalism And The U.N.", Current History, June 1960, Vol. 38, No. 226, pg. 352-258.

Keohane, O. Robert, "The Study Of Political Influence In The General Assembly", International Organization, 1967, Vol. 21, pg. 221-238.

Kerr, Malcolm, "The Middle East Conflict", Foreign Policy Association Headline Series, October 1968, No. 191, pg. 20-28.

Klug, Tony. "The Middle East Conflict: A Tale Of Two Peoples", Young Fabian Pamphlet, January, 1973, No. 32, pg. 10-15

Lande, Gabriella R., "The Effect Of The Resolutions Of The United Nations General Assembly", World Politics, October 1966, Vol, 19, No. 1, pg. 83-106.

Landis, Elizabeth S., "1960 Agenda, Africa - U.N. Report" Africa Today, October, 1960, Vol. 7, No. 6, pg. 11-12.

Legum, Colin, "Israel's Year In Africa: A Study Of Secret Diplomacy", Africa Contemporary Record, 1972, Vol. 3, pg. 1-21.

Manno, Catherine Senf, "Majority Decision And Minority Responses In The U.N. General Assembly", Journal of Conflict Resolution, 1966, Vol. 10, pg. 1

Maslow, Will, "Afro-Asian Bloc In The United Nations", Middle Eastern Affairs, November, 1957, Vol. 8, No. 11, pg. 372-377.

New York Times, February 8, 1970; February 13, 1970; February 17, 1970; April 29, 1971; June 24, 1971; July 11, 1971; May 23, 1975; (News Report)

Rivkin, Arnold, "The U.N. in Africa", West Africa, Part 1, March 26, 1960, No. 2234, p. 353; Part 2, April 2, 1960, No. 2235, p. 376; Part 3, April 9, 1960, No. 2236, p.405.

Sears, Mason, "The Congo, Africa And The U.N.", Africa Today, September, 1960, Vol. 7, No. 5, p. 14-15.

"The U.N. In Africa", West Africa, March 26, 1960, No. 2234, p. 337.

Toure, Sekou, "Call For Real Application Of Right To Self-Determination In Africa", United Nations Review, December, 1959, Vol. 6, No. 6, p. 20-21.

"U.N. Concentrates On Africa", West Africa, December 10, 1960, No. 2271, p. 1409.

Watt, David, "The U.N. And The SmallNations", New Leader, March 6, 1961, Vol. 44, No. 10. p. 6-7.

"West Africans Support U.N.", West Africa, August 27, 1960, No. 2256, p. 975.

Documents

United Nations Document, A/PV. 1468, November 17, 1966,

United Nations Document, A/PV. 1492, December, 1966.

United Nations Document, A/PV. 1562, September 21, 1967.

United Nations Document, A/PV. 1780, October 6, 1969

United Nations Document, A/PV. 1950, October 4, 1971.

United Nations Document, A/PV. 2051, October 3, 1972

United Nations Document, A/PV. 2061, October 10, 1972

United Nations Document, A/PV. 2127, September 25, 1973

United Nations Document, A/PV. 2250, October 1, 1974.

United Nations Document, A/PV. 2296, November 22, 1974.

United Nations Document, A/PV. 2370, October 1, 1975.

United Nations Document, A/PV. 2399, November 10, 1975.

United Nations Document, A/PV. 2400, November 10, 1975.

United Nations Document, A/PV. 9061, May 7, 1973.

United Nations Document, S/11543, October 24, 1974.

United Nations, Proceedings of the U.N. Conference on
Trade and Development, Second Session, Vol. I, Report
and Annexes, 1968.

APPENDIX I

CONTENT ANALYSIS OF GENERAL DEBATE SPEECHES
OF AFRICAN NATIONS IN THE UNITED NATIONS
TWENTY- SECOND ASSEMBLY, 1967
GRAPH - I

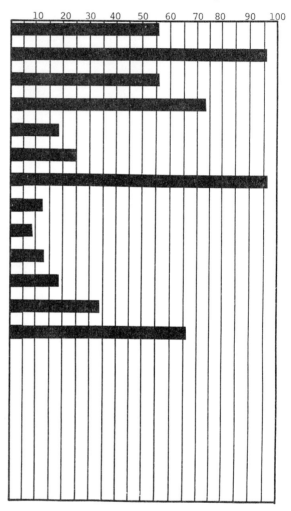

Issue   Per Centage of Nations Raising the Issues

Chinese Representation

Decolonization

Disarmament

Economic Development

Korea

Mercenaries

Middle East

Nigeria-Biafra

Outer Space Technology

Partitioned Country

Refugees

U.N. Organization

Vietnam

152

CONTENT ANALYSIS OF GENERAL DEBATE SPEECHES
OF AFRICAN NATIONS IN THE UNITED NATIONS
TWENTY-THIRD ASSEMBLY, 1968
GRAPH-II

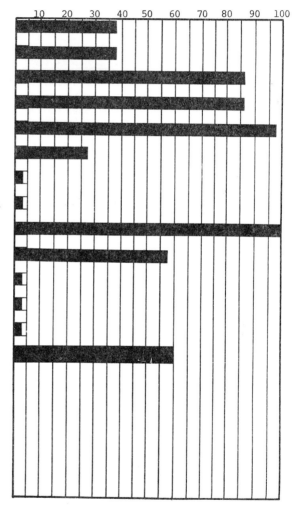

Issues — Per Centage of Nations Raising the Issues

- Chinese Representation
- Czechoslavakia
- Decolonization
- Disarmament
- Economic Development
- Divided Countries (Germany)
- Hijacking
- International Cooperation
- Middle East
- Nigeria - Biafra
- Peace - keeping
- Refugees
- Sea Bed
- Vietnam

CONTENT ANALYSIS OF GENERAL DEBATE SPEECHES
OF AFRICAN NATIONS IN THE UNITED NATIONS
TWENTY - FOURTH ASSEMBLY, 1969
GRAPH - III

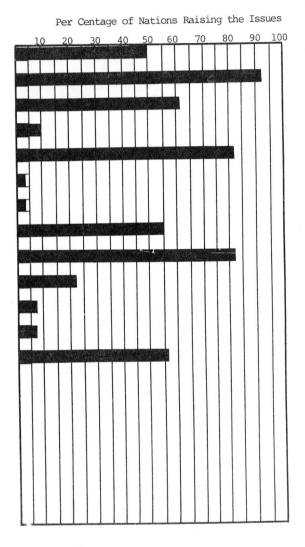

Issues

Per Centage of Nations Raising the Issues

10 20 30 40 50 60 70 80 90 100

Chinese Representation

Decolonization

Disarmament

Divided Countries

Economic Development

Hijacking of Aircraft

International Law

Nigeria-Biafra

Middle East

Korea

Sea - Bed

U.N. Organization

Vietnam

CONTENT ANALYSIS OF GENERAL DEBATE SPEECHES
OF AFRICAN NATIONS IN THE UNITED NATIONS
TWENTY- FIFTH ASSEMBLY, 1970
GRAPH – IV

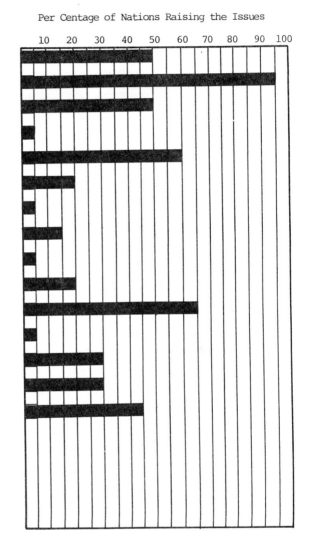

Issues

Per Centage of Nations Raising the Issues

Chinese Representation

Decolonization

Disarmament

Divided Countries

Economic Development

Hijacking of Aircraft

Human Environment

Human Rights

Hunger

Korea

Middle-East

Outlawing War

U.N. Organization

Sea - Bed

Vietnam

CONTENT ANALYSIS OF GENERAL DEBATE SPEECHES
OF AFRICAN NATIONS IN THE UNITED NATIONS
TWENTY- SIXTH ASSEMBLY, 1971
GRAPH - V

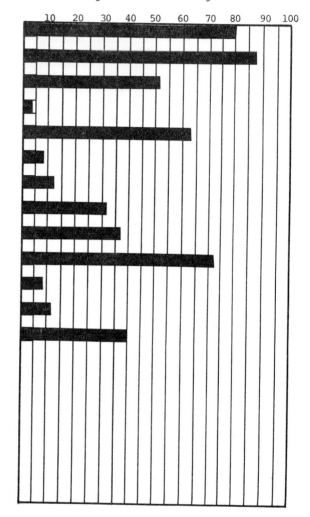

Issues   Per Centage of Nations Raising the Issues

Chinese Representation

Decolonization

Disarmament

Divided Countries

Economic Development

Environment

East Pakistan

Guinea Invasion by
Portugal
Korea

Middle East

U.N. Organization

Sea - Bed

Vietnam

CONTENT ANALYSIS CF GENERAL DEBATE SPEECHES
OF AFRICAN NATIONS IN THE UNITED NATIONS
TWENTY- SEVENTH ASSEMBLY,1972
GRAPH- VI

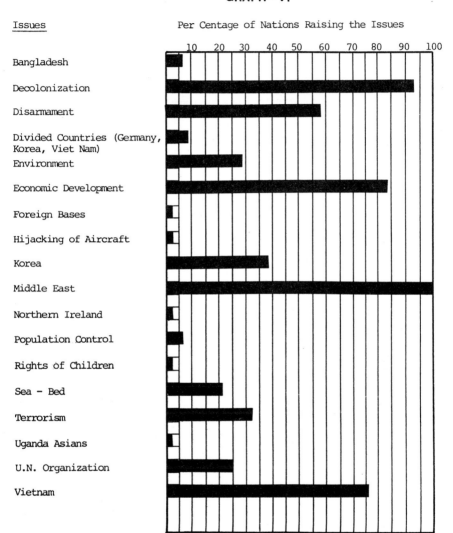

Issues

Per Centage of Nations Raising the Issues

10 20 30 40 50 60 70 80 90 100

Bangladesh

Decolonization

Disarmament

Divided Countries (Germany, Korea, Viet Nam)

Environment

Economic Development

Foreign Bases

Hijacking of Aircraft

Korea

Middle East

Northern Ireland

Population Control

Rights of Children

Sea - Bed

Terrorism

Uganda Asians

U.N. Organization

Vietnam

CONTENT ANALYSIS OF GENERAL DEBATE SPEECHES
OF AFRICAN NATIONS IN THE UNITED NATIONS
TWENTY-EIGHTH ASSEMBLY, 1973
GRAPH -VII

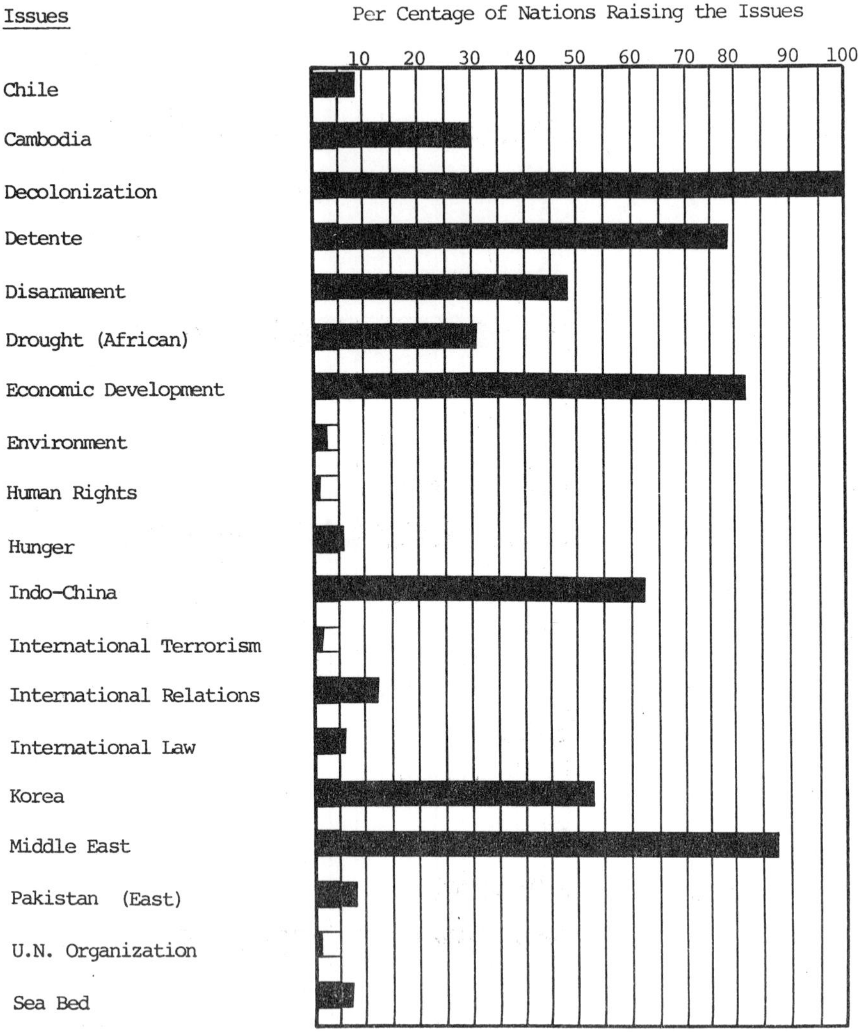

Issues   Per Centage of Nations Raising the Issues

Issue	Per Centage of Nations Raising the Issue
Chile	5
Cambodia	25
Decolonization	100
Detente	75
Disarmament	55
Drought (African)	25
Economic Development	85
Environment	2
Human Rights	2
Hunger	10
Indo-China	70
International Terrorism	2
International Relations	15
International Law	5
Korea	60
Middle East	90
Pakistan (East)	5
U.N. Organization	2
Sea Bed	5

158

CONTENT ANALYSIS OF GENERAL DEBATE SPEECHES
OF AFRICAN NATIONS IN THE UNITED NATIONS
TWENTY- NINTH ASSEMBLY; 1974
GRAPH - VIII

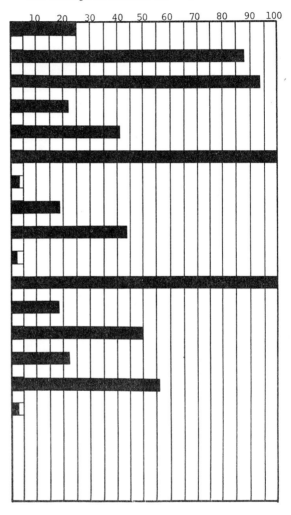

Issues   Per Centage of Nations Raising the Issues

	10	20	30	40	50	60	70	80	90	100

African Drought

Cyprus

Decolonization

Detente

Disarmament

Economic Development

Energy Crisis

Hunger

Korea

Land Locked Countries

Middle East

Population Control

Sea - Bed

Spanish Sahara

South East Asia

U.N. Organization

CONTENT ANALYSIS OF GENERAL DEBATE SPEECHES
OF AFRICAN NATIONS IN THE UNITED NATIONS
THIRTIETH ASSEMBLY, 1975
GRAPH- IX

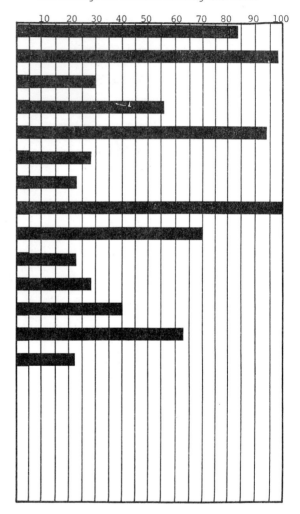

Issues

Per Centage of Nations Raising the Issue

Issues
Cyprus
Decolonization
Detente
Disarmament
Economic Development
Indian Ocean
Int'l Women's Year
Middle East
Korea
Sea - Bed
Spanish Sahara
South East Asia
U.N. Organization
Vietnam

NOTE TO APPENDICES II-IV

   Appendices II-IV contain an analysis of each speech
given by each African delegation in the United Nation's
General Assembly debated from 1967-1975 as to the main issues
raised. The specific position taken on each of these
issues, contained in the column titled "Position Taken".
in each Appendix, refers to a general position of principle,
not specific policy recommendations. The recommendations
of techniques for influencing these issues are noted in the
last column of each Appendix under the column "Type of
Action Suggested". In this column the recommendations are
assigned to categories indicated by abbreviations P for
Persuasion, I for Isolation, MRC for Militant/Radical
Confrontation, NR for No Recommendation. These are
followed by the specific action called for, in parentheses.

   If an African nation chose not to speak for a particular
United Nations session, this is also indicated by "No Speech"
if an african nation gave a speech in the Debate but did not
discuss the issues in question, this is equally indicated by
the notation "No Discussion."

   The General Debate is a standard item on the agenda of the
United Nations for each session, in which every member nation
is given the opportunity to address the world body if it chooses
to do so before the formal business of the session begins. This
is the opportunity for nations to define, discuss, and bring
before the international body those issues which it thinks
confront the world community and deserve some action on the
part of that community.

A P P E N D I X   I I

162

CONTENT ANALYSIS OF THE ISSUE OF DECOLONIZATION FROM THE GENERAL DEBATE SPEECHES OF ALL AFRICAN NATIONS AT THE TWENTY-SECOND SESSION OF THE UNITED NATIONS (1967)

NATION	SPEECHES	FLOOR DISCUSSION OF ISSUE	POSITION TAKEN	TYPES OF ACTION SUGGESTED
Algeria	Speech	X	Favors	NR
Botswana	Speech	X	Favors	NR
Burundi	Speech	X	Favors	I (Deprivations)
Cameroon	Speech	X	Favors	NR
Central African Republic	No Speech			
Chad	Speech	None		
Congo (Brazzaville)	Speech	X	Favors	NR
Congo (Democratic Republic of)	Speech	X	Favors	NR
Dahomey	No Speech			
Ethiopia	Speech	X	Favors	NR
Gabon	Speech	X	Favors	P (Appeal)
Gambia	Speech	X	Favors	I (deprivations)
Ghana	Speech	X	Favors	MRC (Reprisals)
Guinea	No Speech			
Ivory Coast	No Speech			
Kenya	Speech	X	Favors	P (Appeals)
Lesotho	Speech	X	Favors	P (Appeal)
Liberia	Speech	X	Favors	P (Appeal)

163

NATION	SPEECHES	FLOOR DISCUSSION OF ISSUE	POSITION TAKEN	TYPES OF ACTION SUGGESTED
Libya	Speech	X	Favors	NR
Madagascar	Speech	X	Favors	NR
Malawi	Speech	X	Favors	P (Appeal)
Mali	Speech	X	Favors	NR
Mauritania	Speech	X	Favors	P (Appeal)
Morocco	Speech	X	Favors	Appeal
Niger	Speech	None		NR
Nigeria	Speech	X	Favors	P (Appeal)
Rwanda	Speech	X	Favors	P (appeal)
Senegal	Speech	None		NR
Sierra Leone	Speech	X	Favors	P (Appeal)
Somalia	Speech	X	Favors	P (Appeal);
Sudan	Speech	X	Favors	P (Appeal)
Togo	Speech	X	Favors	I (Deprivations)
Tunisia	Speech	X	Favors	P (Appeal)
Uganda	Speech	X	Favors	I (Manadatory Sanctions: Under Chapter 7 of Charter
United Arab Republic	Speech	None		NR
United Republic of Tanzania	Speech	X	Favors	P (Appeal)
Uppoer Volta	Speech	X	Favors	NR

3/Decolonization (1967)

NATION	SPEECHES	FLOOR DISCUSSION OF ISSUE	POSITION TAKEN	TYPES OF ACTION SUGGESTED
Upper Volta	Speech	X	Favors	NR
Zambia	Speech	X	Favors	P (Appeal:Moral Suasion)

CONTENT ANALYSIS OF THE ISSUE OF DECOLONIZATION FROM THE GENERAL DEBATE SPEECHES
OF ALL AFRICAN NATIONS AT THE TWENTY-THIRD SESSION OF THE UNITED NATIONS 1968

NATION	SPEECHES	FLOOR DISCUSSION OF ISSUE	POSITION TAKEN	TYPES OF ACTION SUGGESTED
Algeria	No Speech			NR
Botswana	Speech	X	Favors	P (Appeal)
Burundi	Speech	X	Favors	P (Appeal)
Cameroon	Speech	X	Favors	P (Appeal)
Central African Republic	No Speech			NR
Chad	Speech	X	Favors	P (Negotiation)
Congo (Brazzaville)	No Speech			NR
Congo (Democratic Republic of)	Speech	X	Favors	(Appeal)
Dahomey	No Speech			NR
Equatorial Guinea	No Speech			NR
Ethiopia	Speech	X	Favors	I (Deprivations:
Gabon	Speech	X	Favors	NR
Ghana	Speech	X	Favors	I (Deprivations: Under Chapter 7 of Charter
Guinea	Speech	X	Favors	P (Appeal)
Ivory Coast	No Speech			NR

2/Decolonization (1968)

NATION	SPEECHES	FLOOR DISCUSSION OF ISSUE	POSITION TAKEN	TYPES OF ACTION SUGGESTED
Kenya	Speech	X	Favors	P (Appeal)
Lesotho	Speech	X	Favors	P (Appeal)
Liberia	Speech	X	Favors	NR
Libya	Speech	X	Favors	I (Deprivations)
Madagascar	Speech	X	Favors	P (Appeal:By Example
Malawi	Speech	None		NR
Mali	No Speech			NR
Mauritania	Speech	X	Favors	NR
Morocco	Speech	X	Favors	P (Appeal)
Niger	No Speech			NR
Nigeria	Speech	X	Favors	**NR**
Rwanda	Speech	X	Favors	Negotiations)
Senegal	Speech	X	Favors	NR
Sierra Leone	Speech	X	Favors	P (Appeals)
Somalia	Speech	X	Favors	I (Deprivations)
Sudan	Speech	X	Favors	P (Appeal)
Swaziland	No Speech			NR
Togo	Speech	X	Favors	P (Appeal: Moral Suasion)
Tunisia	Speech	X	Favors	I (Deprivation)

NATION	SPEECHES	FLOOR DISCUSSION OF ISSUE	POSITION TAKEN	TYPES OF ACTION SUGGESTED
Uganda	Speech	X	Favors	P (appeal)
United Arab Republic	Speech	None		NR
United Republic of Tanzania	Speech	X	Favors	I (Deprivation)
Upper Volta	No Speech			NR
Zambia	Speech	X	Favors	P (Appeal)

CONTENT ANALYSIS OF THE ISSUE OF DECOLONIZATION FROM THE GENERAL DEBATE SPEECHES OF ALL AFRICAN NATIONS AT THE TWENTY-FOURTH SESSION OF THE UNITED NATIONS (1969)

NATION	SPEECHES	FLOOR DISCUSSION OF ISSUE	POSITION TAKEN	TYPES OF ACTION SUGGESTED
Algeria	Speech	X	Favors	NR
Botswana	Speech	X	Favors	I (Deprivation: Santion)
Burundi	Speech	X	Favors	P (Appeal)
Cameroon	No Speech			NR
Central African Republic	Speech	X	Favors	MRC (Expulsion of South Africa)
Chad	Speech	X	Favors	P (Appeal)
Congo (Brazzaville)	Speech	X	Favors	NR
Congo (Democratic Republic of)	Speech	X	Favors	P (Negotiation: Lusaka Manifesto
Dahomey	No Speech			NR
Equatorial Guinea	Speech	X	Favors	NR
Ethiopia	Speech	X	Favors	P (Appeal)
Gabon	Speech	X	Favors	NR
Gambia	No Speech			NR
Ghana	No Speech			NR
Guinea	Speech	X	Favors	MRC: (Assist Liberation Movement)

NATIONS	SPEECHES	FLOOR DISCUSSION OF ISSUE	POSITION TAKEN	TYPES OF ACTION SUGGESTED
Ivory Coast	Speech	X	Favors	P (Appeal)
Kenya	Speech	X	Favors	I (Deprivations: Sanctions)
Lesotho	No Speech	X		NR
Liberia	Speech	X	Favors	NR
Madagascar	Speech	X	Favors	NR
Malawi	No Speech			NR
Mali	Speech	X	Favors	P (Negotiation)
Mauritania	Speech	X	Favors	P (Negotiation: Support Lusaka Manifesto)
Maurituis	No Speech			NR
Morocco	Speech	X		NR
Niger	No Speech		Favors	MPC (Support the Armed Struggles of Africans in Southern. Africa
Rwanda	Speech	X	Favors	NR
Senegal	Speech	X	Favors	P (Negotiation)
Sierra Leone	Speech	X	Favors	MRC (Violence)
Somalia	Speech	X	Favors	I (Deprivations: Sanctions)
Sudan	Speech	X	Favors	NR

3/Decolonization (1969)

NATION	SPEECHES	FLOOR DISCUSSION OF ISSUE	POSITION TAKEN	TYPES OF ACTION SUGGESTED
Swaziland	Speech	X	Favors	NR
Togo	No Speech			NR
Tunisia	Speech	X	Favors	NR
Uganda	Speech	X	Favors	NR
United Arab Republic	Speech	X	Favors	NR
Upper Volta	Speech	X	Favors	(Measures in Articles 41 & 42 of U.N. Charter)
United Republic of Tanzania	Speech	X	Favors	MRC (Support Armed Struggle)
Zaire	Speech	X	Favors	P (Negotiations: Lusaka Manifesto)
Zambia	Speech	X	Favors	MRC (Force Under Articles 41 & 42

CONTENT ANALYSIS OF THE ISSUE OF DECOLONIZATION FROM THE GENERAL DEBATE SPEECHES
OF ALL AFRICAN NATIONS AT THE TWENTY-FIFTH SESSION OF THE UNITED NATIONS (1970)

NATION	SPEECHES	FLOOR DISCUSSION OF ISSUE	POSITION TAKEN	TYPES OF ACTION SUGGESTED
Algeria	Speech	X	Favors	MRC (Strengthen National Liberation Movements)
Botswana	No Speech			NR
Burundi	No Speech			NR
Cameroon	Speech	None		NR
Central African Republic	No Speech			NR
Chad	No Speech			NR
Congo (democratic Republic of)	No Speech			NR
Dahomey	No Speech			NR
Equatorial Guinea	No Speech			NR
Ethiopia	No Speech			NR
Gabon	No Speech			NR
Gambia	Speech	X	Favors	MRC (Under Chapter II, ART. 6 of Charter Expulsion of Portugal)
Ghana	Speech	X	Favors	P

2/Decolonization (1970)

NATION	SPEECHES	FLOOR DISCUSSION OF ISSUE	POSITION TAKEN	TYPES OF ACTION SUGGESTED
Guinea	Speech	X	Favors	P (Appeal: Lusaka Manifesto)
Ivory Coast	No Speech			NR
Kenya	Speech	X	Favors	I (Deprivations)
Lesotho	No Speech			NR
Liberia	Speech	X	Favors	NR
Libya	Speech	X	Favors	MRC (Support of Liberation Move- ments
Madagascar	Speech	None		NR
Malawi	No Speech			NR
Mali	No Speech			NR
Mauritania	No Speech			NR
Morocco	Speech	X	Favors	MRC (Material Support for Liberation Move- ment
Niger	No Speech			NR
Nigeria	No Speech			NR
People's Republic of the Congo	Speech	X	Favors	MRC (Support Armed Struggle)

NATION	SPEECHES	FLOOR DISCUSSION OF ISSUE	POSITION TAKEN	TYPES OF ACTION SUGGESTED
Rwanda	Speech		Favors	P(Negotiation: Lusaka Manifesto)
Senegal	No Speech			NR
Sierra Leone	Speech	X	Favors	MRC (Support Freedom Fighters)
Somalia	Speech	X	Favors	NR
Sudan	Speech	X	Favors	MRC(Use Force Measures Provided Under Article 41 of U.N. Charter)
Swaziland	No Speech			NR
Togo	Speech	X	Favors	I(Sanctions6)
Tunisia	Speech	X	Favors	MRC
Uganda	No Speech	X		NR
United Arab Republic	No Speech			NR
United Republic of Tanzania	No Speech			NR
Upper Volta	No Speech			NR
Zambia	No Speech	x	Favors	I(Mandatory Sanctions As Provided Under Chapter 7 of Charter

CONTENT ANALYSIS OF THE ISSUE OF DECOLONIZATION FROM THE GENERAL DEBATE SPEECHES
OF ALL AFRICAN NATIONS AT THE TWENTY-SIXTH SESSION OF THE UNITED NATIONS (1971)

NATION	SPEECHES	FLOOR DISCUSSION OF ISSUE	POSITION TAKEN	TYPES OF ACTION SUGGESTED
Algeria	Speech	X	Favors	NR
Botswana	No Speech	X	Favors	P (Negotiations)
Burundi	No Speech			NR
Cameroon	Speech	X	Favors	P(Negotiation: Lusaka Manifesto)
Central African Republic	Speech	X	Favors	P(Negotiation)
Chad	Speech	X	Favors	NR
Congo	Speech	X	Favors	NR
Dahomey	Speech	X		NR
Egypt	Speech	X	Favors	I(Deprivations)
Equatorial Guinea	No Speech			NR
Ethiopia	No Speech	X		NR
Gabon	Speech	X	Favors	NR
Gambia	No Speech	X		NR
Ghana	Speech	X	Favors	P(Negotiation: Lusaka Manifesto

175

2/Decolonization (1971)

NATION	SPEECH	FLOOR DISCUSSION OF ISSUE	POSITION TAKEN	TYPES OF ACTION SUGGESTED
Guinea	Speech	X	Favors	MRS(Reprisals)
Ivory Coast	Speech	X	Favors	P(Negotiations)
Kenya	Speech	X	Favors	P (Appeal)
Lesotho	No Speech			NR
Liberia	Speech	X	Favors	NR
Libyan Arab Republic	Speech	X	Favors	MRC(Expulsion of S. Africa From All Int'l. Directions)
Madagascar	Speech	X	Favors	P(Negotiation)
Malawi	No Speech			NR
Mali	Speech	X	Favors	I(Sanctions:Provision of Chapter 7 of U.N. Charter)
Mauritania	Speech	X	Favors	MRC(Violence and Support of Liberation Movement)
Niger	Speech	X	Favors	P(Appeal)
Nigeria	Speech	X	Favors	NR

3/Decolonization (1971)

NATION	SPEECHES	FLOOR DISCUSSION OF ISSUE	POSITION TAKEN	TYPES OF ACTION SUGGESTED
Rwanda	Speech	X	Favors	NR
Senegal	Speech	X	Favors	NR
Sierra Leone	Speech	X	Favors	I (Deprivations)
Somalia	Speech	X	Favors	NR
Sudan	Speech	X	Favors	P(Appeal)
Swaziland	No Speech	X	Favors	I (Deprivations)
Togo	Speech	X	Favors	I (Deprivations)
Tunisia	Speech	None		NR
Uganda	Speech	X	Favors	P(appeals)
United Republic of Tanzania	Speech	X	Favors	MRC(Outlaw South Africans From The Community of Nations)
Upper Volta	Speech	X	Favors	MRC(Moral and Material Support to Liberation Movement)
Zaire	No Speech			NR
Zambia	Speech	X	Favors	MRC(Moral and Material Support of Liberation Movement)

CONTENT ANALYSIS OF THE ISSUE OF DECOLONIZATION FROM THE GENERAL DEBATE SPEECHES OF ALL AFRICAN NATIONS AT THE TWENTY-**SEVENTH SESSION** OF **THE** UNITED NATIONS (1972)

NATION	SPEECHES	FLOOR DISCUSSION OF ISSUE	POSITION TAKEN	TYPES OF ACTION SUGGESTED
Algeria	Speech	X	Favors	P (Negotiation)
Botswana	No Speech			NR
Burundi	Speech	X	Favors	MRC(Expulsion of Colonialist Nation Under Article 6 of U.N. Charter)
Cameroon	Speech	X	Favors	MRC(Moral and Material Support of Liberation Movements)
Central African Republic	Speech	X	Favors	P (Appeal))
Chad	Speech	X	Favors	NR
Congo	Speech	X	Favors	MRC(Military Force)
Dahomey	Speech	X	Favors	P (Appeal)
Egypt	Speech	X	Favors	NR
Equatorial Guinea	No Speech			NR
Ethiopia	Speech	X	Favors	I (Deprivations)
Gabon	Speech	X	Favors	P (Appeal)

2/Decolonization (1972)

NATION	SPEECHES	FLOOR DISCUSSION OF ISSUE	POSITION TAKEN	TYPES OF ACTION SUGGESTED
Gambia	Speech	X	Favors	P (Negotiation)
Ghana	Speech	X	Favors	MRC(Moral and Material Liberation Movement
Ivory Coast	Speech	X	Favors	P (Negotiation)
Kenya	Speech	X	Favors	I (Deprivations)
Lesotho	No Speech			NR
Liberia	Speech	X	Favors	MRC (Reprisals)
Libya	Speech	None		NR
Madagascar	Speech	X	Favors	NR
Malawi	Speech	X	Favors	P (Negotiation)
Mali	Speech	X	Favors	MRC (Material Support of Liberation Movement)
Mauritania	Speech	X	Favors	NR
Morocco	Speech	X	Favors	MRC(Support Liberation Movement)
Niger	Speech	X	Favors	I (Deprivations)
Nigeria	Speech	X	Favors	MRC (Force)

NATION	SPEECHES	FLOOR DISCUSSION OF ISSUE	POSITION TAKEN	TYPES OF ACTION SUGGESTED
People's Republic of Congo	No Speech			NR
Rwandi	Speech	X	Favors	P (Appeal)
Senegal	Speech	X	Favors	I (Sanctions Under Chapter 7 of U.N. Charter)
Sierra Leone	Speech	X	Favors	I (Deprivations)
Somalia	Speech	X	Favors	MRC (Reprisals)
Sudan	Speech	X	Favors	NR
Swaziland	Speech	None		NR
Togo	Speech	X	Favors	MRC (Reprisals)
Tunisia	Speech	X	Favors	P (Negotiation)
Uganda	Speech	None		NR
United Republic of Tanzania	Speech	X	Favors	MRC (Reprisals)
Upper Volta	Speech	X	Favors	MRC (Reprisals)
Zaire	Speech	X	Favors	P (Appeal)
Zambia	Speech	X	Favors	MRC (Reprisals)

CONTENT ANALYSIS OF THE ISSUE OF DECOLONIZATION FROM THE GENERAL DEBATE SPEECHES OF ALL AFRICAN NATIONS AT THE TWENTY-EIGHTH SESSION OF THE UNITED NATIONS (1973)

NATION	SPEECHES	FLOOR DISCUSSION OF ISSUE	POSITION TAKEN	TYPES OF ACTION SUGGESTED
Algeria	Speech	X	Favors	I(Sanctions:Economic Measures Designed to Break Resistance)
Botswana	No Speech			NR
Burundi	Speech	X	Favors	MRC(Expulsion of Portugal from U.N.)
Cameroon	No Speech			NR
Central African Republic	Speech	X	Favors	NR
Chad	No Speech			NR
Congo	Speech	X	Favors	P(Appeal)
Dahomey	Speech	X	Favors	P (Negotiation)
Egypt	Speech	None		NR
Equatorial Guinea	Speech	None		NR
Ethiopia	Speech	X	Favors	MRC(Material Support to Liberation Struggle)
Gabon	Speech	X	Favors	NR
Gambia	No Speech			NR

181

2/Decolonization (1973)

NATION	SPEECHES	FLOOR DISCUSSION OF ISSUE	POSITION TAKEN	TYPES OF ACTION SUGGESTED
Ghana	Speech	X	Favors	MRC(Material Assistance to Armed Struggle)
Guinea	Speech	X	Favors	MRC(Rejection of Credentials of South Africa to U.N.)
Ivory Coast	No Speech			NR
Kenya	Speech	X	Favors	MRC(Expulsion of Portugal from U.N.)
Lesotho	Speech	X	Favors	MRC(Assistance to Liberation Struggles)
Liberia	Speech	X	Favors	MRC(Render Material Assistance to Liberation Struggle)
Libya	Speech	X	Favors	MRC(Assist Liberation Movement)
Madagascar	Speech	X	Favors	NR
Malawi	No Speech			NR
Mali	Speech	X	Favors	I(Sanctions)
Mauritania	Speech	X	Favors	NR
Morocco	Speech	X	Favors	NR

3/Decolonization (1973)

NATION	SPEECHES	FLOOR DISCUSSION OF ISSUE	POSITION TAKEN	TYPES OF ACTION SUGGESTED
Niger	Speech	X	Favors	(P) Appeal
Nigeria	Speech	X	Favors	MRC (Material Assistance to Liberation Movements)
People's Republic of Congo	No Speech			
Rwanda	Speech	X	Favors	NR
Senegal	Speech	X	Favors	MRC(Rejection of South Africa's Credentials to U.N.)
Sierra Leone	Speech	X	Favors	I(Sanctions: In Travel, Communication Sports, Political, Economic and Cultural Activities)
Somalia	Speech	X	Favors	MRC(Assistance to Armed Struggle)
Sudan	Speech	X	Favors	NR
Swaziland	No Speech			NR
Togo	No Speech			NR
Tunisia	Speech	None		NR
Uganda	No Speech			NR
United Republic of Tanzania	Speech	X	Favors	MRC(Material Support for Liberation Movement and Rejection)

4/Decolonization (1973)

NATION	SPEECHES	FLOOR DISCUSSION OF ISSUE	POSITION TAKEN	TYPES OF ACTION SUGGESTED
United Republic con't.				of South Africa's Credentials to U.N.)
Upper Volta	Speech	X	Favors	P(Appeal)
Zaire	Speech	X	Favors	MRC(Assistance to Liberation Movement)
Zambia	Speech	X	Favors	MRC(Material Assistance to Liberation Movement

184

CONTENT ANALYSIS OF THE ISSUE OF DECOLONIZATION FROM THE GENERAL DEBATE SPEECHES OF ALL AFRICAN NATIONS AT THE TWENTY- NINTH SESSION OF THE UNITED NATIONS (1974)

NATION	SPEECHES	FLOOR DISCUSSION OF ISSUE	POSITION TAKEN	TYPES OF ACTION SUGGESTED
Algeria	Speech	X	Favors	NR
Botswana	Speech	X	Favors	P (Appeal)
Burundi	Speech	X	Favors	(MRC (Expulsion of South Africa's Credentials to U.N.)
Cameroon	Speech	X	Favors	MRC(Challenge to South Africa's Membership to U.N.)
Central African Republic	Speech	X	Favors	MRC(Challenge South Africa's Membership to U.N.)
Chad	Speech	X	Favors	P (Appeal)
Congo	Speech	X	Favors	P (Appeal)
Dahomey	Speech	X	Favors	MRC(Expulsion of South Africa's Membership to U. N.)
Egypt	Speech	None		NR
Equatorial Guinea	Speech	X	Favors	MRC(Recognition of Liberation Movements)
Ethiopia	Speech	X	Favors	MRC(Challenge South Africa's Membership to U.N.)

2/Decolonization (1974)

NATION	SPEECHES	FLOOR DISCUSSION OF ISSUE	POSITION TAKEN	TYPES OF ACTION SUGGESTED
Gabon	Speech	X	Favors	NR
Gambia	Speech	X	Favors	P (Negotiation)
Ghana	Speech	X	Favors	P (Appeal)
Guinea	Speech	X	Favors	NR
Ivory Coast	Speech	X	Favors	P (Appeal)
Kenya	Speech	X	Favors	I(Sanctions: Arms Embargo and Termination of Diplomatic Commercial and Consular Relations with South Africa)
Lesotho	Speech	X	Favors	MRC(Material Assistance to Armed Struggle)
Liberia	Speech	X	Favors	MRC(Challenge South Africa's Membership to U.N.)
Libya	Speech	X	Favors	MRC(Challenge South Africa's Membership to U.N.)
Madagascar	No Speech			NR
Malawi	No Speech			NR
Mali	Speech	X	Favors	NR
Mauritania	Speech	X	Favors	NR
Morocco	Speech	X	Favors	NR
Niger	Speech	X	Favors	P (Appeal)

3/Dec olonization (1974)

NATION	SPEECHES	FLOOR DISCUSSION OF ISSUE	POSITION TAKEN	TYPES OF ACTION SUGGESTED
Nigeria	Speech	X	Favors	NR
People's Republic of Congo	No Speech	None		NR
Rwanda	Speech	X	Favors	NR
Senegal	Speech	X	Favors	NR
Sierra Leone	Speech	X	Favors	I(Sanctions: Boycott of South Africa's Travel, Communication Sports, Cultural, Political and Economic Activites)
Somalia	No Speech			NR
Sudan	No Speech			Nr
Swaziland	Speech	X	Favors	P(Appeal)
Togo	Speech	X	Favors	NR
Tunisia	Speech	X	Favors	NR
Uganda	Speech	X	Favors	MRC(Expulsion of South African from U.N.)
United Republic of Tanzania	Speech	X	Favors	MRC(Expulsion of South Africa from U.N.)
Upper Volta	Speech	X	Favors	NR
Zaire	Speech	X	Favors	P (Appeal)
Zambia	Speech	X	Favors	P (Negotiaton)

CONTENT ANALYSIS OF THE ISSUE OF DECOLONIZATION FROM THE GENERAL DEBATE SPEECHES OF ALL AFRICAN NATIONS AT THE **THIRTIETH** SESSION OF THE UNITED NATIONS (1975)

NATION	SPEECHES	FLOOR DISCUSSION OF ISSUE	POSITION TAKEN	TYPES OF ACTION SUGGESTED
Algeria	Speech	X	Favors	NR
Botswana	No Speech			Nr
Burundi	No Speech			NR
Cameroon	Speech	X	Favors	MRC(Support Liberation Movement)
Central African Republic	No Speech			NR
Chad	Speech	X	Favors	NR
Congo	Speech	X	Favors	MRC(Armed Struggles)
Dahomey	Speech	X	Favors	NR
Democratic Rep. of Soa Tome and Principle	No Speech			NR
Egypt	No Speech			NR
Ethiopia	No Speech			NR
Gabon	Speech	X	Favors	NR
Gambia	No Speech			NR
Ghana	Speech	X	Favors	I(Comprehensive Sanctions)
Guinea	No Speech			NR
Ivory Coast	No Speech			NR
Kenya	Speech	X	Favors	MRC(Asst. Armed Struggles)
Lesotho	Speech	X	Favors	NR

2/Decolonization (1975)

NATION	SPEECHES	FLOOR DISCUSSION OF ISSUE	POSITION TAKEN	TYPES OF ACTION SUGGESTED
Liberia	Speech	X	Favors	P (Negotiation)
Libya	Speech	X	Favors	NR
Madagascar	Speech	X	Favors	NR
Malawi	No Speech			NR
Mali	Speech	X	Favors	NR
Mauritania	Speech	X	Favors	NR
Morocco	Speech	X	Favors	NR
Niger	No Speech			NR
Nigeria	Speech	X	Favors	MRC(Support National Liberation Movement)
People's Republic of Congo	No Speech			NR
People's Republic of Mozambique	Speech	X	Favors	MRC(Support Liberation Movement)
Republic of Cape Verde	No Speech			NR
Rwanda	Speech	X	Favors	MRC(Expulsion of South Africa from UN
Senegal	Speech	X	Favors	MAC(Support Liberation Movement)
Sierra Leone	Speech	X	Favors	I (Sanctions)

NATION	SPEECHES	FLOOR DISCUSSION OF ISSUE	POSITION TAKEN	TYPES OF ACTION SUGGESTED
Somalia	Speech	X	Favors	MRC(All Coercive Measures Under Charter and Support Liberation Movement)
Sudan	Speech	X	Favors	NR
Swaziland	No Speech			NR
Togo	Speech	X	Favors	P (Negotiation)
Tunisia	Speech	X	Favors	I (Deprivations)
Uganda	Speech	X	Favors	MRC (Support Liberation Movement)
United Republic of Tanzania	Speech	X	Favors	MRC(Expulsion of South African from All International Organizations)
Upper Volta	Speech	X	Favors	NR
Zaire	Speech	X	Favors	NR
Zambia	Speech	X	Favors	MRC (Armed Struggle)

A P P E N D I X I I I

191

CONTENT ANALYSIS OF THE ISSUE OF MIDDLE EAST FROM THE GENERAL DEBATE SPEECHES
OF ALL AFRICAN NATIONS AT THE TWENTY-SECOND SESSION OF THE UNITED NATIONS (1967)

NATION	SPEECHES	FLOOR DISCUSSION OF ISSUE	POSITION TAKEN	TYPES OF ACTION SUGGESTED
Algeria	Speech	X	Territorial Integrity	NR
Botswana	Speech	X	Territorial Integrity	P (Negotiation)
Burundi	Speech	X	Territorial Integrity	NR
Cameroon	Speech	X	Territorial Integrity	P (Appeal)
Central African Republic	No Speech			
Chad	Speech	X	Territorial Integrity	P (Negotiation)
Congo (Brazzaville)	Speech	X	Territorial Integrity	P (Appeal)
Congo (Democratic Repulbic of)	Speech	X	Territorial Integrity	P (Negotiation)
Dahomey	No Speech		Territorial Integrity	P (Negotiation)
Ethiopia	Speech	X	Territorial Integrity	P (Negotiation)
Gabon	Speech	X	Territorial Integrity	P (Appeal)

2/Middle East (1967)

NATION	SPEECHES	FLOOR DISCUSSION OF ISSUE	POSITION TAKEN	TYPES OF ACTION SUGGESTED
Gambia	Speech	X	Territorial Integrity	NR
Ghana	Speech	X	Territorial Integrity	P (Negotiation)
Guinea	No Speech			NR
Ivory Coast	No Speech			NR
Kenya	Speech	X	Territorial Integrity	P (Negotiation)
Lesotho	Speech	X	Territorial Integrity	NR
Liberia	Speech	X	Territorial Integrity	NR P (Negotiation)
Libya	Speech	X	Territorial Integrity	NR
Madagascar	Speech	X	Territorial Integrity	P (Negotiation)
Malawi	Speech	X	Territorial Integrity	P (Negotiation)
Mali	Speech	X	Territorial Integrity	NR
Mauritania	Speech	X	Territorial Integrity	NR
Morocco	Speech	X	Territorial Integrity	P (Appeal)

NATION	SPEECHES	FLOOR DISCUSSION OF ISSUE	POSITION TAKEN	TYPES OF ACTION SUGGESTED
Niger	Speech	None	Territorial Integrity	NR
Nigeria	Speech	X	Territorial Integrity	NR
Rwanda	Speech	X	Territorial Integrity	P (Negotiation)
Senegal	Speech	X	Territorial Integrity	P (Appeal)
Sierra Leonne	Speech	X	Territorial Integrity	P (Negotiation)
Somalia	Speech	X	Territorial Integrity	(P(Negotiation)
Sudan	Speech	X	Territorial Integrity	NR
Togo	Speech	X	Territorial Integrity	P (Negotiation)
Tunisia	Speech	X	Territorial Integrity	NR
Uganda	Speech	X	Territorial Integrity	P (Negotiation)
United Arab Republic	Speech	x	Territorial Integrity	P (Appeal)
United Republic of Tanzania	Speech	X	Territorial Integrity	P (Appeal)

4/Middle East (1967)

NATION	SPEECHES	FLOOR DISCUSSION OF ISSUE	POSITION TAKEN	TYPES OF ACTION SUGGESTED
Upper Volta	Speech	X	Territorial	P (Negotiation)
Zambia	Speech	X	Territorial Integrity	NR

CONTENT ANALYSIS OF THE ISSUE OF THE MIDDLE EAST FROM THE GENERAL DEBATE SPEECHES
OF ALL AFRICAN NATIONS AT THE TWENTY-THIRD SESSION OF THE UNITED NATIONS (1968)

NATION	SPEECHES	FLOOR DISCUSSION OF ISSUE	POSITION TAKEN	TYPES OF ACTION SUGGESTED
Algeria	No Speech			NR
Botswana	Speech	None		NR
Burundi	Speech	X	Territorial Integrity	P (Appeal)
Cameroon	Speech	X	Territorial Integrity	P (Appeal)
Central African Republic	No Speech			NR
Chad	Speech	X	Territorial Integrity	P (Negotiation)
Congo (Brazzaville)	No Speech			NR
Congo (Democratic Republic of)	Speech	X	Territorial Integrity	NR
Dahomey	No Speech		Territorial Integrity	NR NR
Equatorial Guinea	No Speech			NR
Ethiopia	Speech	X	Territorial Integrity	P (Negotiation)
Gabon	Speech	X	Territorial Integrity	NR
Gambia	Speech	X	Territorial Integrity	P (Negotiation)

2/Middle East (1968)

NATION	SPEECHES	FLOOR DISCUSSION OF ISSUE	POSITION TAKEN	TYPES OF ACTION SUGGESTED
Ghana	Speech	X	Territorial Integrity	P (Negotiation)
Guinea	Speech	X	Territorial Integrity	P (Negotiation)
Ivory Coast	No Speech			NR
Kenya	Speech	X	Territorial Integrity	P (Negotiation)
Lesotho	Speech	X	Territorial Integrity	P (Negotiation)
Libya	Speech	X	Territorial Integrity	NR
Madagascar	Speech	X	Territorial Integrity	P (Appeal)
Malawi	Speech	X	Territorial Integrity	P (Negotiation)
Mali	No Speech			NR
Mauritania	Speech	X	Territorial Integrity	NR
Morocco	Speech	X	Territorial Integrity	P (Appeal)
Niger	No Speech			NR
Nigeria	Speech	X	Territorial Integrity	P (Negotiation)
Rwanda	Speech	X	Territorial Integrity	P (Negotiation)

3/Middle East (1968)

NATION	SPEECHES	FLOOR DISCUSSION OF ISSUE	POSITION TAKEN	TYPES OF ACTION SUGGESTED
Senegal	Speech	X	Territorial Integrity	P (Negotiation)
Sierra Leone	Speech	X	Territorial Integrity	P (Negotiation)
Somalia	Speech	X	Territorial Integrity	P (Negotiation)
Sudan	Speech	X	Territorial Integrity	NR
Swaziland	No Speech		Territorial Integrity	NR
Togo	Speech	X	Territorial Integrity	NR
Tunisia	Speech	X	Territorial Integrity	P (Negotiation)
Uganda	Speech	X	Territorial Integrity	P (Negoitiation)
United Arab Republic	Speech	X	Territorial Integrity	P (Negotiation)
United Republic of Tanzania	Speech	X	Territorial Integrity	P (Appeal)
Upper Volta	No Speech		Territorial Integrity	NR
Zambia	Speech	X	Territorial Integrity	P (Negotiation)

CONTENT ANALYSIS OF THE ISSUE OF THE MIDDLE EAST FROM THE GENERAL DEBATE SPEECHES OF ALL AFRICAN NATIONS AT THE TWENTY-FOURTH SESSION OF THE UNITED NATIONS (1969)

NATION	SPEECHES	FLOOR DISCUSSION OF ISSUE	POSITION TAKEN	TYPES OF ACTION SUGGESTED
Algeria	Speech	X	None	NR
Botswana	Speech	No		NR
Burundi	Speech	X	Territorial Integrity	P (Appeal)
Cameroon	No Speech			NR
Central African Republic	Speech	No		NR
Chad	Speech	X	Territorial Integrity	P (Negotiation)
Congo (Brazzaville)	Speech	X	Territorial Integrity	NR
Congo (Democratic Republic of)	Speech	X	Territorial Integrity	P (negotiation)
Dahomey	No Speech			NR
Equatorial Guinea	Speech	X	None	P (Negotiation)
Ethiopia	Speech	X	Territorial Integrity	P (Appeal)
Gabon	Speech	X	Territorial Integrity	P (Negotiation)
Gambia	No Speech			
Ghana	No Speech			NR
Guinea	Speech	X	Territorial Integrity	NR
Ivory Coast	Speech	X	NONE	NR

NATION	SPEECHES	FLOOR DISCUSSION OF ISSUE	POSITION TAKEN	TYPES OF ACTION SUGGESTED
Kenya	Speech	X	Territorial Integrity	P (Appeal)
Lesotho	No Speech			NR
Liberia	Speech	X	Territorial Integrity	NR
Libya	Speech	X	Territorial Integrity	NR
Madagascar	No Speech			NR
Malawi	No Speech			NR
Mali	Speech	X		NR
Mauritania	Speech	X	Territorial Integrity	MRC(Material and Moral Support of Pa Palestinian Liberation)
Mauritius	No Speech			NR
Morocco	Speech	X	Territorial Integrity	P (Appeal)
Niger	No Speech			NR
Nigeria	Speech	X	Territorial Integrity	P (negotiation)
Rwanda	Speech	X	Territorial Integrity	P (Negotiation)
Senegal	Speech	X	Territorial Integrity	P (Appeal)
Sierra Leone	Speech	X	Territorial Integrity	P (Negotiation)
Somalia	Speech	X	Territorial Integrity	I Sanctions)

3/Middle East (1969)

NATION	SPEECHES	FLOOR DISCUSSION OF ISSUE	POSITION TAKEN	TYPES OF ACTION SUGGESTED
Sudan	Speech	X	Territorial Integrity	NR
Swaziland	Speech	X	Territorial Integrity	NR
Togo	No Speech			NR
Tunisia	Speech	X	Territorial Integrity	P (Negotiation)
Uganda	Speech	X	None	NR
United Arab Republic	Speech	X	Territorial Integrity	P (Negotiation)
United Republic of Tanzania	Speech	X	Territorial Integrity	P (Negotiation)
Upper Volta	Speech	X	Territorial Integrity	P (Negotiation)
Zambia	Speech	X	Territorial Integrity	P (Negotiation)

CONTENT ANALYSIS OF THE ISSUE OF THE MIDDLE EAST FROM THE GENERAL DEBATE SPEECHES
OF ALL AFRICAN NATIONS AT THE TWENTY-FIFTH SESSION OF THE UNITED NATIONS (1970)

NATION	SPEECHES	FLOOR DISCUSSION OF ISSUE	POSITION TAKEN	TYPES OF ACTION SUGGESTED
Algeria	Speech	X	Territorial Integrity	MRC(Stengthen National Liberation Movement)
Botswana	No Speech			NR
Burundi	No Speech			NR
Cameroon	Speech	None		NR
Central African Republic	No Speech			NR
Chad	No Speech			NR
Congo (Democratic Republic of	No Speech			NR
Dahomey	No Speech			NR
Equatorial Guinea	No Speech			NR
Ethiopia	No Speech			NR
Gabon	No Speech			NR
Gambia	Speech	X	Territorial Integrity	P (Negotiation)
Ghana	Speech	X	Territorial Integrity	P (Negotiation
Guinea	Speech	X	Territorial Integrity	P (Negotiation)
Ivory Coast	No Speech			NR
Kenya	Speech	X	Territorial Integrity	P (Negotiation)
Lesotho	No Speech			NR

2/Middle East (1970)

NATION	SPEECHES	FLOOR DISCUSSION OF ISSUE	POSITION TAKEN	TYPES OF ACTION SUGGESTED
Liberia	Speech	X	Territorial Integrity	P (Negotiation: Roger Plan)
Libya	Speech	X	None	
Madagascar	Speech	None		NR
Malawi	No Speech			NR
Mali	No Speech			NR
Mauritania	No Speech			NR
Morocco	Speech	X	Territorial Integrity	P (Negotiation)
Niger	No Speech			NR
Nigeria	No Speech			NR
People's Republic of the Congo	Speech	X	Territorial Integrity	P (Negotiation)
Rwanda	Speech	X	Territorial Integrity	P (Negotiation)
Senegal	No Speech			NR
Sierra Leone	Speech	X	Territorial Integrity	P (Negotiation)
Somalia	Speech	X	Territorial Integrity	NR

203

NATION	SPEECHES	FLOOR DISCUSSION OF ISSUE	POSITION TAKEN	TYPES OF ACTION SUGGESTED
Sudan	Speech	X	Territorial Integrity	NR
Swaziland	No Speech			NR
Togo	Speech	X	Territorial Integrity	P (Negotiation: Roger Plan)
Tunisia	Speech	X	Territorial Integrity	P (Negotiation)
Uganda	No Speech		Territorial Integrity	NR
United Arab Republic	No Speech			NR
United Republic of Tanzania	No Speech			NR
Upper Volta	No Speech			NR
Zambia	Speech	X	Territorial Integrity	P (Negotiation)

CONTENT ANALYSIS OF THE ISSUE OF THE MIDDLE EAST FROM THE GENERAL DEBATE SPEECHES
OF ALL AFRICAN NATIONS AT THE TWENTY-SIXTH SESSION OF THE UNITED NATIONS (1971)

NATION	SPEECHES	FLOOR DISCUSSION OF ISSUE	POSITION TAKEN	TYPES OF ACTION SUGGESTED
Algeria	Speech	X	None	P (Negotiation)
Botswana	No Speech			NR
Burundi	No Speech			NR
Cameroon	Speech	X	Territorial Integrity	P (Negotiation)
Central African Republic	Speech	X	Territorial Integrity	P (Negotiation: OAU Mission)
Chad	Speech	X	Territorial Integrity	P (Negotiation: OAU Committee)
Congo	Speech	X	Territorial Integrity	P (Negotiation: OAU Committee)
Dahomey	Speech	X	None	P (Negotiation)
Egypt	Speech	X	Territorial Integrity	P (Negotiation: OAU Committee)
Equatorial Guinea	No Speech			
Ethiopia	Speech	X	Territorial Integrity	P (Negotiation)
Gabon	Speech	X	Territorial Integrity	P (Negotiation: Reactivate Jarring Mission)

NATION	SPEECHES	FLOOR DISCUSSION OF ISSUE	POSITION TAKEN	TYPES OF ACTION SUGGESTED
Gambia	No Speech			NR
Ghana	Speech	X	Territoral Integrity	NR
Guinea	Speech	X	Territorial Integrity	NR
Ivory Coast	Speech	X	Territorial Integrity	P (negotiation)
Kenya	Speech	X	Territorial	P (Negotiation: OAU Committee)
Lesotho	No Speech			NR
Liberia	Speech	X	None	P (Negotiation: OAU Committee)
Libyan Arab Republic	Speech	X	Territorial Integrity	NR
Madagascar	Speech	X	Territorial Integrity	P (Negotiation)
Malawi	No Speech			NR
Mali	Speech	X	Territorial Integrity	P (Negotiation)
Mauritania	Speech	X	Territorial Integrity	P (Negotiation: Jarring Mission & OAU Committee)

3/Middle East 1971

NATION	SPEECHES	FLOOR DISCUSSION OF ISSUE	POSITION TAKEN	TYPES OF ACTION SUGGESTED
Morocco	Speech	x	Territorial Integrity	(P (Appeal)
Niger	Speech	X	Territorial Integrity	P (Negotiation) African Mission
Nigeria	Speech	x	Territorial Integrity	P (Negotiation OAU Committee)
Rwanda	Speech	X	Territorial Integrity	P (Negotiation Jarring Mission)
Senegal	Speech	No	Territorial Integrity	NR
Sierra Leone	Speech	X	Territorial Integrity	P (Negotiation OAU Committee)
Somalia	Speech	X	Territorial Integrity	P (Negotiation
Sudan	Speech	X	Territorial Integrity	NR
Swaziland	No Speech			NR
Togo	Speech	X	Territorial	P (Negotiation African Mission)
Tunisia	Speech	X	Territorial Integrity	NR
Uganda	Speech	X	Territorial	P (Negotiation: OAU Committee)
United Republic of Tanzania	Speech	X	Territorial Integrity	NR

4/Middle East 1971

NATION	SPEECHES	FLOOR DISCUSSION OF ISSUE	POSITION TAKEN	TYPES OF ACTION SUGGESTED
Upper Volta	Speech	X	Territorial Integrity	P (Negotiation: Jarring Mission)
Zaire	No Speech			
Zambia	Speech	X	Territorial Integrity	P (Negotiation: OAU Committee)

CONTENT ANALYSIS OF THE ISSUE OF THE MIDDLE EAST FROM THE GENERAL DEBATE SPEECHES
OF ALL AFRICAN NATIONS AT THE TWENTY-SEVENTH SESSION OF THE UNITED NATIONS (1972)

NATION	SPEECHES	FLOOR DISCUSSION OF ISSUE	POSITION TAKEN	TYPES OF ACTION SUGGESTED
Algeria	Speech	X	Territorial Integrity	NR
Botswana	No Speech			NR
Burundi	Speech	X	Territorial Integrity	NR
Cameroon	Speech	X	Territorial Integrity	P (Negotiation)
Central African Republic	Speech	X	Territorial Integrity	P (Negotiation Resumption of Jarring Mission)
Chad	Speech	X	Territorial Integrity	NR
Congo	Speech	None		NR
Dahomey	Speech	X	Territorial Integrity	P (Negotiation)
Egypt	Speech	X	Territorial Integrity	P (Negotiation)
Equatorial Guinea	No Speech			NR
Ethiopia	Speech	X	Territorial Integrity	P (Negotiation)
Gabon	Speech	X	Territorial Integrity	P (Negotiation)
Gambia	Speech	None	Territorial Integrity	NR

NATION	SPEECHES	FLOOR DISCUSSION OF ISSUE	POSITION TAKEN	TYPES OF ACTION SUGGESTED
Ghana	Speech	X	Territorial Integrity	NR
Guinea	Speech	x	Territorial Integrity	P (Appeal)
Ivory Coast	Speech		None	P (Negotiation)
Kenya	Speech	X	Territorial Integrity	NR
Lesotho	No Speech			NR
Liberia	Speech	X	Territorial Integrity	P (Negotiation: Jarring Mission)
Libya	Speech	None		P (Appeal)
Madagascar	Speech	X	None	NR
Malawi	Speech	None		NR
Mali	Speech	X	Territorial Integrity	NR
Mauritania	Speech	X	Territorial Integrity	P (Negotiation)
Morocco	Speech	X	None	NR
Niger	Speech	X	Territorial Integrity	P (Negotiation)
Nigeria	Speech	X	Territorial Integrity	P (Negotiation)

3/Middle East (1972)

NATION	SPEECHES	FLOOR DISCUSSION OF ISSUE	POSITION TAKEN	TYPES OF ACTION SUGGESTED
People's Republic of the Congo	No Speech		Territorial Integrity	NR
Rwanda	Speech	X	Territorial Integrity	P (Negotiation)
Senegal	Speech	X	Territorial Integrity	P (Negotiation)
Sierre Leone	Speech	X	Territorial Integrity	P (Negotiation)
Somalia	Speech	X	Territorial Integrity	NR
Sudan	Speech	X	None	NR
Swaziland	Speech	X	None	NR
Togo	Speech	X	Territorial Integrity	P (Negotiation)
Tunisia	Speech	X	None	NR
Uganda	Speech	None		NR
United Republic of Tanzania	Speech	X	Territorial Integrity	P (Negotiation)
Upper Volta	Speech	X	Territorial Integrity	P (Negotiation)
Zaire	Speech	X	Territorial Integrity	NR
Zambia	Speech	X	Territorial Integrity	P (Negotiation)

CONTENT ANALYSIS OF THE ISSUE OF THE MIDDLE EAST FROM THE GENERAL DEBATE SPEECHES
OF ALL AFRICAN NATIONS AT THE TWENTY-EIGHT SESSION OF THE UNITED NATIONS (1973)

NATION	SPEECHES	FLOOR DISCUSSION OF ISSUE	POSITION TAKEN	TYPES OF ACTION SUGGESTED
Algeria	Speech	X	Territorial Integrity	I (Sanctions: Political and Economic Measures Against Israel)
Botswana	No Speech			NR
Burundi	Speech	X		P Negotiation
Cameroon	No Speech		Territorial Integrity	NR
Central African Republic	Speech	None		NR
Chad	No Speech			NR
Congo	Speech	X	Territorial Integrity	I (Break Diplomatic Relations with Israel)
Dahomey	Speech	X	Territorial Integrity	NR
Egypt	Speech	X	Territorial Integrity	NR
Equatorial Guinea	Speech	None	Territorial Integrity	NR
Ethiopia	Speech	X	Territorial Integrity	NR
Gabon	Speech	X	Territorial	P (Negotiation: Restore Jarring Misson)

2/Middle East (1973)

NATION	SPEECHES	FLOOR DISCUSSION OF ISSUE	POSITION TAKEN	TYPES OF ACTION SUGGESTED
Gambia	No Speech			NR
Ghana	Speech	X	None	NR
Guinea	Speech	X	Territorial Integrity	NR
Ivory Coast	No Speech			NR
Kenya	Speech	X	Territorial Integrity	P (Negotiation: Fresh African Initiative)
Lesotho	Speech	X	Territorial Integrity	MRC (Material and Political Assistance to Palestinian People
Liberia	Speech	X	Territorial Integrity	P (Negotiation)
Libya	Speech	X	None	MRC (Support Palestinian Struggle)
Madagascar	Speech	X	None	NR
Malawi	No Speech			NR
Mali	Speech	X	Territorial Integrity	NR
Mauritania	Speech	X	Territorial Integrity	NR
Morocco	Speech	X	Territorial Integrity	NR
Niger	Speech	X	Territorial Integrity	I (Breaking of Diplomatic Relations with Israel.)

213

NATION	SPEECHES	FLOOR DISCUSSION OF ISSUE	POSITION TAKEN	TYPES OF ACTION SUGGESTED
Nigeria	Speech	X	Territorial Integrity	NR
People's Republic of Congo	No Speech			NR
Rwanda	Speech	X	Territorial Integrity	P (Negotiation)
Senegal	Speech	X	Territorial Integrity	NR
Sierra Leone	Speech	X	Territorial Integrity	NR
Somalia	Speech	X	Territorial Integrity	I (Breaking of Diplomatic Relations with Israel)
Sudan	Speech	X	None	NR
Swaziland	No Speech			NR
Togo	No Speech			NR
Tunisia	Speech	X	None	NR
Uganda	No Speech			NR
United Republic of Tanzania	Speech	X	Territorial Integrity	NR
Upper Volta	Speech	X	Territorial Integrity	NR
Zaire	Speech	X	Territorial Integrity	I (Breaking of Diplomatic Relations with Israel)

4/Middle East (1973)

NATION	SPEECHES	FLOOR DISCUSSION OF ISSUE	POSITION TAKEN	TYPES OF ACTION SUGGESTED
Zambia	Speech	X	Territorial Integrity	NR

CONTENT ANALYSIS OF THE ISSUE OF THE MIDDLE EAST FROM THE GENERAL DEBATE SPEECHES
OF ALL AFRICAN NATIONS AT THE TWENTY-NINTH SESSION OF THE UNITED NATIONS (1974)

N ATION	SPEECHES	FLOOR DISCUSSION OF ISSUE	POSITION TAKEN	TYPES OF ACTION SUGGESTED
Algeria	Speech	X	None	NR
Botswana	Speech	X	Territorial Integrity	NR
Burundi	Speech	X	Territorial Integrity	MRC(Recognize Palestine Liberation Organization)
Cameroon	Speech	X	Territorial Integrity	P (Negotiation)
Central African Republic	Speech	X	Territorial Integrity	NR
Chad	Speech	X	Territorial Integrity	NR
Congo	Speech	X	None	NR
Dahomey	Speech	X	Territorial Integrity	P (Negotiation)
Egypt	Speech	X	Territorial Integrity	MRC(Recognize Palestine Liberation Organization)
Equatorial Guinea	Speech	X	Territorial Integrity	NR
Ethiopia	Speech	X	Territorial Integrity	NR
Gabon	Speech	None		
Gambia	Speech	X	Territorial Integrity	NR

2/Middle East (1974)

NATION	SPEECHES	FLOOR DISCUSSION OF ISSUE	POSITION TAKEN	TYPES OF ACTION SUGGESTED
Ghana	Speech	X	Territorial Integrity	P (Negotiation)
Guinea	Speech	X	Territorial Integrity	NR
Ivory Coast	Speech	X	Territorial Integrity	P (Negotiation)
Kenya	Speech	X	Territorial Integrity	P (Negotiation)
Lesotho	Speech	X	Territorial Integrity	NR
Liberia	Speech	X	Territorial Integrity	P(Negotiation:Resume Geneva Conference)
Libya	Speech	X	None	MRC(Recognition of Representative of Palestinians)
Madagascar	No Speech			NR
Malawi	No Speech			NR
Mali	Speech	X	Territorial Integrity	NR
Mauritania	Speech	X	Territorial Integrity	MRC(Recognize Palestine Liberation Organization)
Morocco	Speech	X	Territorial Integrity	MRC(Recognize Palestine Liberation Organization)
Niger	Speech	X	Territorial Integrity	NR

3/Middle East (1974)

NATION	SPEECHES	FLOOR DISCUSSION OF ISSUE	POSITION TAKEN	TYPES OF ACTION SUGGESTED
Nigeria	Speech	X	None	NR
People's Republic of Congo	No Speech			NR
Rwanda	Speech	X	None	NR
Senegal	Speech	X	Territorial Integrity	P (Negotiation: Geneva Conference)
Sierra Leone	Speech	X	Territorial Integrity	NR
Somalia	No Speech		Territorial Integrity	NR
Sudan	No Speech			NR
Swaziland	Speech	X	None	P(Negotiation)
Togo	Speech	X	Territorial Integrity	P (Negotiation)
Tunisia	Speech	X	Territorial Integrity	MRC(Recognition of Palestine Liberation Organization)
Uganda	Speech	X	Territorial Integrity	NR
United Republic of Tanzania	Speech	X	Territorial	MRC(Recognize PLO)
Upper Volta	Speech	X	Territorial Integrity	P (Negotiation)
Zaire	Speech	X	None	NR
Zambia	Speech	X	Territorial Integrity	P(Negotiation:Geneva Talks)

NATION	SPEECHES	FLOOR DISCUSSION OF ISSUE	POSITION TAKEN	TYPES OF ACTION SUGGESTED
Guinea	No Speech			NR
Ivory Coast	No Speech			NR
Kenya	Speech	X	Territorial Integrity	P(Negotiation)
Lesotho	Speech	X	Territorial Integrity	P (Negotiation)
Liberia	Speech	X	Territorial Integrity	NR
Libya	Speech	X	Territorial Integrity	NR
Madagascar	Speech	X	Territorial Integrity	NR
Malawi	No Speech			NR
Mali	Speech	X	Territorial Integrity	NR
Mauritania	Speech	X	Territorial Integrity	NR
Morocco	Speech	X	Territorial Integrity	NR
Niger	No Speech			NR
Nigeria	Speech	X	None	P (Negotiation)
People's Republic of Congo	No Speech			NR
People's Republic of Mozambique	Speech	X	Territorial Integrity	P(Negotiation)

NATION	SPEECHES	FLOOR DISCUSSION OF ISSUE	POSITION TAKEN	TYPES OF ACTION SUGGESTED
Republic of Cape Verde	No Speech		Territorial Integrity	NR
Rwanda	Speech	X	Territorial Integrity	P(Negotiation)
Senegal	Speech	X	Territorial Integrity	NR
Sierra Leone	Speech	X	Territorial Integrity	P(Negotiation)
Somalia	Speech	X	Territorial Integrity	MRC(Expulsion of Israel from U.N. and Force)
Sudan	Speech	X	Territorial Integrity	NR
Swaziland	No Speech		Territorial Integrity	P (Negotiation)
Togo	Speech	X	Territorial Integrity	P (Negotiation)
Tunisia	Speech	X	Territorial Integrity	P (Negotiation)
Uganda	Speech	X	Territorial Integrity	MRC(Expulsion of Israel from UN)
United Republic of Tanzania	Speech	X	Territorial Integrity	MRC(Support Resistance of PLO)
Upper Volta	Speech	X	Territorial Integrity	NR
Zaire	Speech	X	Territorial Integrity	I(Deprivations:Break Relations with Israel
Zambia	Speech	X	Territorial Integrity	NR

220

APPENDIX IV

221

CONTENT ANALYSIS OF THE ISSUE OF THE ECONOMIC DEVELOPMENT FROM THE GENERAL DEBATE SPEECHES
OF ALL AFRICAN NATIONS AT THE TWENTY-SECOND SESSION OF THE UNITED NATIONS (1967)

NATION	SPEECHES	FLOOR DISCUSSION OF ISSUE	POSITION TAKEN	TYPES OF ACTION SUGGESTED
Algeria	Speech	X	Favors	P (appeal)
Botswana	Speech	X	Favors	P (Appeal)
Burundi	Speech	X	Favors	P (Appeal)
Cameroon	Speech	X	Favors	P (Appeal)
Central African Republic	No Speech			
Chad	Speech	X	Favors	NR
Congo (Braxxaville)	Speech	X	Favors	P (Appeal)
Congo (Democratic Republic of)	Speech	X	Favors	P (Appeal)
Dahomey	No Speech			NR
Ethiopia	Speech	X	Favors	P (Appeal
Gabon	Speech	X	Favors	P (Appeal)
Gambia	Speech	X	Favors	P (Appeal)
Ghana	Speech	X	Favors	P (Appeal)
Guinea	No Speech			NR
Ivory Coast	No Speech			NR

2/Economic Development (1967)

NATION	SPEECHES	FLOOR DISCUSSION OF ISSUE	POSITION TAKEN	TYPES OF ACTION SUGGESTED
Kenya	Speech	None		NR
Lesotho	Speech	X	Favors	P (Appeal
Liberia	Speech	X	Favors	P (Appeal
Libya	Speech	X	Favors	P(Appeal)
Madagascar	Speech	X	Favors	NR
Malawi	Speech	X	None	NR
Mali	Speech	None		NR
Mauritania	Speech	None		NR
Morocco	Speech	X	Favors	P (Appeal)
Niger	Speech	X	Favors	P (Appeal)
Nigeria	Speech	X	Favors	P (Appeal)
Rwanda	Speech	X	Favors	P (Appeal)
Senegal	Speech	None		NR
Sierra Leone	Speech	X	Favors	NR
Somalia	Speech	None		NR
Sudan	Speech	X	Favors	P (Appeal)
Togo	Speech	X	Favors	P (Appeal)
Tunisia	Speech	x	Favors	P (Appeal)

223

3/Economic Development (1967)

NATION	SPEECHES	FLOOR DISCUSSION OF ISSUE	POSITION TAKEN	TYPES OF ACTION SUGGESTED
Uganda	Speech	X	Favors	P (Appeal)
United Arab Republic	Speech	None		NR
United Republic of Tanzania	Speech	X	Favors	P (Appeal)
Upper Volta	Speech	X	Favors	P (Appeal)
Zambia	Speech	None		NR

CONTENT ANALYSIS OF THE ISSUE OF THE ECONOMIC DEVELOPMENT FROM THE GENERAL DEBATE
SPEECHES OF ALL AFRICAN NATIONS AT THE TWENTY-THIRD SESSION OF THE UNITED NATION (1968)

NATION	SPEECHES	FLOOR DISCUSSION OF ISSUE	POSITION TAKEN	TYPES OF ACTION SUGGESTED
Algeria	No Speech			NR
Botswana	Speech	X	Favors	P (Appeal)
Burundi	Speech	X	Favors	P (Appeal)
Cameroon	Speech	X	Favors	NR
Central African Republic	No Speech			NR
Chad	No Speech			NR
Congo (Brazzaville)	No Speech			NR
Congo (Democratic Republic of)	Speech	X	Favors	P (Appeal
Dahomey	No Speech			NR
Equatorial Guinea	No Speech			NR
Ethiopia	Speech	X	Favors	P (Appeal)
Gabon	Speech	X	Favors	P (Appeal)
Gambia	No Speech			NR
Ghana	Speech	X	Favors	P (Appeal)
Guinea	Speech	X	Favors	P (Appeal)

225

NATION	SPEECHES	FLOOR DISCUSSION OF ISSUE	POSITION TAKEN	TYPES OF ACTION SUGGESTED
Ivory Coast	No Speech			NR
Senegal	Speech	X	Favors	P(Appeal)
Lesotho	Speech	X	Favors	P (Appeal)
Liberia	Speech	X	Favors	P (Appeal
Libya	Speech	X	Favors	NR
Madagascar	Speech	X	Favors	P (Appeal)
Malawi	Speech	None		NR
M li	No Speech			NR
Mauritania	No Speech			NR
Morocco	Speech	X	Favors	P (Appeal)
Niger	No Speech			NR
Nigeria	Speech	X	Favors	P (Appeal)
Rwanda	Speech	X	Favors	P (Appeal)
Senegal	Speech	X	Favors	P (Appeal)
Sierra Leone	Speech	None		NR
Somalia	Speech	X	Favors	P (Appeal)
Sudan	Speech	X	Favors	P (Appeal)
Swaziland	No Speech			NR

226

3/Economic Development (1968)

NATION	SPEECHES	FLOOR DISCUSSION OF ISSUE	POSITION TAKEN	TYPES OF ACTION SUGGESTED
Togo	Speech	X	Favors	P (Appeal)
Tunisia	Speech	X	Favors	P (Appeal)
Uganda	Speech	X	Favors	P (Appeal)
United Arab Republic	Speech	None		NR
United Republic of Tanzania	Speech	X	Favors	P (Appeal)
Upper Volta	No Speech			NR
Zambia	Speech	None		NR

227

CONTENT ANALYSIS OF THE ISSUE OF THE ECONOMIC DEVELOPMENT FROM THE GENERAL DEBATE SPEECHES
OF ALL AFRICAN NATIONS AT THE TWENTY-FOURTH SESSION OF THE UNITED NATIONS (1969)

NATION	SPEECHES	FLOOR DISCUSSION OF ISSUE	POSITION TAKEN	TYPES OF ACTION SUGGESTED
Algeria	Speech	X	Favors	P (Appeal)
Botswana	Speech	X	Favors	NR
Burundi	Speech	X	Favors	P (Appeal)
Cameroon	No Speech			NR
Central African Republic	Speech	X	Favors	P (Appeal)
Chad	Speech	X	Favors	P (Appeal)
Congo (Brazzaville)	Speech	X	Favors	P (Appeal)
Congo (Democratic Republic)	Speech	X	Favors	P (Appeal)
Dahomey	No Speech			NR
Equatorial Guinea	Speech	None		NR
Ethiopia	Speech	X	Favors	P (Appeal)
Gabon	No Speech			NR
Gambia	No Speech			NR
Ghana	No Speech			NR
Guinea	Speech	X	Favors	P (Appeal)
Ivory Coast	Speech	X	Favors	P (Appeal)

2/Economic Development (1969)

NATION	SPEECHES	FLOOR DISCUSSION OF ISSUE	POSITION TAKEN	TYPES ACTION SUGGESTED
Kenya	Speech	X	Favors	P (Appeal)
Lesotho	No Speech			NR
Liberia	Speech	X	Favors	P (Appeal)
Libya	Speech	None		NR
Madagascar	No Speech			NR
Malawi	No Speech			NR
Mali	Speech	X	Favors	P (Appeal)
Mauritania	Speech	X	Favors	P (Appeal)
Mauritus	No Speech			NR
Morocco	Speech	X	Favors	P Appeal
Niger	No Speech			NR
Nigeria	Speech	X	Favors	P (Appeal)
Rwanda	Speech	X	Favors	P (Appeal)
Senegal	Speech	X	Favors	P (Appeal)
Sierra Leone	Speech	X	Favors	P (Appeal)
Somalia	Speech	None		NR
Sudan	Speech	X	Favors	NR
Swaziland	Speech	X	Favors	NR

NATION	SPEECHES	FLOOR DISCUSSION OF ISSUE	POSITION TAKEN	TYPES OF ACTION SUGGESTED
Togo	No Speech			NR
Tunisia	Speech	X	Favors	P Appeal
Uganda	Speech	X	Favors	P (Appeal)
United Arab Republic	Speech	X	Favors	NR
United Republic of Tanzania	Speech	X	Favors	P (Appeal)
Upper Volta	Speech	X	Favors	P (Appeal)
Zambia	Speech	X	Favors	P (Appeal)

CONTENT ANALYSIS OF THE ISSUE OF THE ECONOMIC DEVELOPMENT FROM THE GENERAL DEBATE SPEECHES

OF ALL AFRICAN NATIONS AT THE TWENTY-FIFTH SESSION OF THE UNITED NATIONS (1970)

NATION	SPEECHES	FLOOR DISCUSSION OF ISSUE	POSITION TAKEN	TYPES OF ACTION SUGGESTED
Algeria	Speech	X	Favors	P (Appeal)
Botswana	No Speech			NR
Burundi	No Speech			NR
Cameroon	Speech	None		NR
Central African Republic	No Speech			NR
Chad	No Speech			NR
Congo (Democratic Republic of)	No Speech			NR
Dahomey	No Speech			NR
Equatorial Guinea	No Speech			NR
Ethiopia	No Speech			NR
Gabon	No Speech			NR
Gambia	Speech	None		NR
Ghana	Speech	X	Favors	P (Appeal)
Guinea	Speech	X	Favors	P (Appeal)
Ivory Coast	No Speech			NR
Kenya	Speech	X	Favors	P (Appeal)
Lesotho	No Speech			NR
Liberia	Speech	X	Favors	P (Appeal)

231

2/Economic Development (1970)

NATIONS	SPEECHES	FLOOR DISCUSSION OF ISSUE	POSITION TAKEN	TYPES OF ACTION SUGGESTED
Libya	Speech	X	Favors	NR
Madagascar	Speech	None		NR
Malawi	No Speech			NR
Mali	No Speech			NR
Mauritania	No Speech			NR
Morocco	Speech	None		NR
Niger	No Speech			NR
Nigeria	No Speech			NR
People's Republic of Congo	Speech		Favors	P (Appeal)
Rwanda	Speech	X	Favors	P (Appeal)
Senegal	No Speech			NR
Sierra Leone	Speech	X	Favors	P (Appeal)
Somalia	Speech	None		NR
Sudan	Speech	None	NR	NR
Swaziland	No Speech			NR
Togo	Speech	X	Favors	P (Appeal)
Tunisia	Speech	X	Favors	P (Appeal)

3/Economic Development (1970)

NATION	SPEECHES	FLOOR DISCUSSION OF ISSUE	POSITION TAKEN	TYPES OF ACTION SUGGESTED
Uganda	No Speech			NR
United Arab Republic	No Speech			NR
United Republic of Tanzania	No Speech			NR
Upper Volta	No Speech			NR
Zambia	Speech	X	Favors	P (Appeal)

CONTENT ANALYSIS OF THE ISSUE OF THE ECONOMIC DEVELOPMENT FROM THE GENERAL DEBATE
SPEECHES OF ALL AFRICAN NATIONS AT THE TWENTY-SIXTH SESSION OF THE UNITED NATIONS (1971)

NATION	SPEECHES	FLOOR DISCUSSION OF ISSUE	POSITION TAKEN	TYPES OF ACTION SUGGESTED
Algeria	Speech	X	Favors	P (Appeal)
Botswana	No Speech			NR
Burundi	No Speech			NR
Cameroon	Speech	X	Favors	P (Negotiation)
Central African Republic	Speech	X	Favors	P (Appeal)
Chad	Speech	X	Favors	P (Appeal)
Congo	Speech	X	Favors	P (Negotiation)
Dahomey	Speech	X	Favors	P (Appeal)
Egypt	Speech	None		NR
Ethiopia	Speech	X	Favors	P (Appeal)
Equatorial Guinea	No Speech			NR
Gabon	Speech	X	Favors	P (Appeal)
Gambia	No Speech			NR
Ghana	Speech	None		NR
Guinea	Speech	X	Favors	P Appeal)
Ivory Coast	Speech	X	Favors	P (Appeal)
Kenya	Speech	X	Favors	P (Appeal)
Lesotho	No Speech			NR

2/Economic Development (1971)

NATION	SPEECHES	FLOOR DISCUSSION OF ISSUE	POSITION TAKEN	TYPES OF ACTION SUGGESTED
Liberia	Speech	X	Favors	P (Appeal)
Libyan Arab Republic	Speech	None		NR
Madagascar	Speech	X	Favors	P (Appeal)
Malawi	No Speech			NR
Mali	No Speech			NR
Mauritania	Speech	X	Favors	P (Appeal)
Morocco	Speech	X	Favors	P (Appeal)
Niger	Speech	X	Favors	P (Appeal)
Nigeria	Speech	X	Favors	P (Appeal)
People's Republic of Congo	Speech	X	Favors	P (Appeal)
Rwanda	Speech	X	Favors	P (Appeal)
Senegal	Speech	X	Favors	NR
Sierra Leone	Speech	X	Favors	P (Appeal)
Somalia	Speech	X	Favors	NR
Sudan	Speech	X	Favors	NR
Swaziland	No Speech			NR
Togo	Speech	X	Favors	P (Appeal)
Tunisia	Speech	None		NR

235

3/Economic Development (1971)

NATION	SPEECHES	FLOOR DISCUSSION OF ISSUE	POSITION TAKEN	TYPES OF ACTION SUGGESTED
Uganda	Speech	X	Favors	P (Appeal)
United Republic of Tanzania	Speech	X	Favors	P (Appeal)
Upper Volta	Speech	X	Favors	P (Appeal)
Zaire	No Speech			NR
Zambia	Speech	X	Favors	P (Appeal)

CONTENT ANALYSIS OF THE ISSUE OF THE ECONOMIC DEVELOPMENT FROM THE GENERAL DEBATE SPEECHES
OF ALL AFRICAN NATIONS AT THE TWENTY-SEVENTH SESSION OF THE UNITED NATIONS (1972)

NATIONS	SPEECHES	FLOOR DISCUSSION OF ISSUE	POSITION TAKEN	TYPES OF ACTION SUGGESTED
Algeria	Speech	X	Favors	NR
Botswana	No Speech			NR
Burundi	Speech	X	Favors	P (Appeal)
Cameroon	Speech	X	Favors	P (Appeal)
Central African Republic	Speech	X	Favors	P (Appeal)
Chad	Speech	X	Favors	P (Appeal)
Congo	Speech	X	Favors	P (Appeal)
Dahomey	Speech	X	Favors	P (Appeal)
Egypt	Speech	X	Favors	P (Appeal)
Equatorial Guinea	No Speech			
Ethiopia	Speech	X	Favors	NR
Gabon	Speech	X	Favors	NR
Gambia	Speech	X	Favors	NR
Ghana	Speech	X	Favors	P (Appeal)
Guinea	Speech	X	Favors	P (Appeal)
Ivory Coast	Speech	X	Favors	P (Appeal)
Kenya	Speech	X	Favors	P (Appeal)

237

2/Economic Development (1972)

NATION	SPEECHES	FLOOR DISCUSSION OF ISSUE	POSITION TAKEN	TYPES OF ACTION SUGGESTED
Lesotho	No Speech		NR	NR
Liberia	Speech	X	Favors	P (Appeal)
Libya	Speech	None	NR	NR
Madagasacr	Speech	X		NR
Malawi	Speech	None		NR
Mali	Speech	X	Favors	NR
Mauritania	Speech	X	Favors	NR
Morocco	Speech	None		NR
Niger	Speech	X	Favors	P (Appeal)
Nigeria	Speech	X	Favors	P (Appeal)
People's Republic of Congo	No Speech		NR	NR
Rwanda	Speech	X	Favors	P (Appeal)
Senegal	Speech	X	Favors	P (Appeal)
Sierra Leone	Speech	X	Favors	P (Appeal)
Somalia	Speech	X	Favors	P (Appeal)
Sudan	Speech	X	Favors	P Appeal
Swaziland	Speech	X	Favors	P (Appeal)
Togo	Speech	X	Favors	P (Appeal)
Tunisia	Speech	None	Favors	P (Appeal)

238

3/Economic Development (1972)

NATION	SPEECHES	FLOOR DISCUSSION OF ISSUE	POSITION TAKEN	TYPES OF ACTION SUGGESTED
Uganda	Speech	None		NR
United Republic of Tanzania	Speech	X	Favors	P (Appeal)
Upper Volta	Speech	X	Favors	NR
Zaire	Speech	X	Favors	P (Appeal)
Zambia	Speech	X	Favors	P (Appeal)

239

CONTENT ANALYSIS OF THE ISSUE OF THE ECONOMIC DEVELOPMENT FROM THE GENERAL DEBATE SPEECHES
OF ALL AFRICAN NATIONS AT THE TWENTY-EIGTH SESSION OF THE UNITED NATIONS (1973)

NATION	SPEECHES	FLOOR DISCUSSION OF ISSUE	POSITION TAKEN	TYPES OF ACTION SUGGESTED
Algeria	Speech	X	Favors	P (Appeal)
Botswana	No Speech			NR
Burundi	Speech	X	Favors	P (Appeal)
Cameroon	No Speech			NR
Central African Republic	Speech	None		NR
Chad	No Speech	None		NR
Congo	Speech	X	Favors	P (Appeal)
Dahomey	Speech	X	Favors	P (Appeal)
Egypt	Speech	None		NR
Equatorial Guinea	Speech	X	Favors	P (Appeal)
Ethiopia	Speech	X	Favors	NR
Gabon	Speech	X	Favors	NR
Gambia	No Speech			NR
Ghana	Speech	X	Favors	P (Appeal)
Guinea	Speech	X	Favors	P (Appeal)
Ivory Coast	No Speech			NR
Kenya	Speech	None		

240

2/Economic Development (1973)

NATION	SPEECHES	FLOOR DISCUSSION OF ISSUE	POSITION TAKEN	TYPES OF ACTION SUGGESTED
LLesotho	Speech	X	Favors	P (Appeal)
Liberia	Speech	X	Favors	P (Appeal)
Libya	Speech	None		NR
Madagascar	Speech	X	Favors	P (Appeal)
Malawi	No Speech			NR
Mali	Speech	X	Favors	P (Appeal)
Mauritania	Speech	X	Favors	P (Appeal)
Morocco	Speech	None		NR
Niger	Speech	None		NR
Nigeria	Speech	X	Favors	P (Appeal)
People's Republic of Congo	No Speech			NR
Rwanda	Speech	X	Favors	P (Appeal)
Senegal	Speech	X	Favors	P (Appeal)
Sierra Leone	Speech	X	Favors	NR
Somalia	Speech	None		
Sudan	Speech	X	Favors	P (Appeal)
Swaziland	No Speech			NR
Togo	No Speech			NR
Tunisia	Speech	None		NR

241

3/Economic Development (1973)

NATION	SPEECHES	FLOOR DISCUSSION OF ISSUE	POSITION TAKEN	TYPES OF ACTION SUGGESTED
Uganda	No Speech			NR
United Republic of Tanzania	Speech	X	Favors	P (Appeal)
Upper Volta	Speech	X	Favors	P (Appeal)
Zaire	Speech	X	Favors	P (Appeal)
Zambia	Speech	X	Favors	P (Appeal)

CONTENT ANALYSIS OF THE ISSUE OF THE ECONOMIC DEVELOPMENT FROM THE GENERAL DEBATE SPEECHES
OF ALL AFRICAN NATIONS AT THE TWENTY-NINTH SESSION OF THE UNITED NATIONS (1974)

NATION	SPEECHES	FLOOR DISCUSSION OF ISSUE	POSITION TAKEN	TYPES OF ACTION SUGGESTED
Algeria	Speech	X	Favors	P (Appeal)
Botswana	Speech	X	Favors	P (Appeal)
Burundi	Speech	X	Favors	P (Negotiation)
Cameroon	Speech	X	Favors	P (Appeal)
Central African Republic	Speech	X	Favors	P (Appeal)
Chad	Speech	X	Favors	P (Appeal)
Congo	Speech	X	Favors	P (Negotiation)
Dahomey	Speech	X	Favors	P (Appeal)
Egypt	Speech	None		NR
Equatorial Guinea	Speech	X	Favors	P (Appeal)
Ethiopia	Speech	X	Favors	P (Appeal)
Gabon	Speech	X	Favors	P (Appeal)
Gambia	Speech	X	Favors	P (Appeal)
Ghana	Speech	X	Favors	P (Appeal)
Guinea	Speech	X	Favors	P (Appeal)
Ivory Coast	Speech	X	Favors	P (Appeal)
Kenya	Speech	X	Favors	P (Appeal)
Lesotho	Speech	X	Favors	P (Appeal)
Liberia	Speech	X	Favors	P (Appeal)

243

NATION	SPEECHES	FLOOR DISCUSSION OF ISSUE	POSITION TAKEN	TYPES OF ACTION SUGGESTED
Libya	Speech	X	Favors	P (Appeal)
Madagascar	No Speech			NR
Malawi	No Speech			NR
Mali	Speech	X	Favors	P (Appeal)
Mauritania	Speech	X	Favors	P (Appeal)
Morocco	Speech	X	Favors	P (Appeal)
Niger	Speech	None		NR
Nigeria	Speech	X	Favors	P (Appeal)
People's Republic of Congo	No Speech			NR
Rwanda	Speech	X	Favors	P Appeal
Senegal	Speech	X	Favors	P (Appeal)
Sierra Leone	Speech	X	Favors	P (Appeal)
Somalia	No Speech			NR
Sudan	No Speech			NR
Swaziland	Speech	X	Favors	P Appeal
Togo	Speech	X	Favors	P (Appeal)
Tunisia	Speech	X	Favors	P (Appeal)
Uganda	Speech	X	Favors	P (Appeal)

3/Economic Development (1974)

NATION	SPEECHES	FLOOR DISCUSSION OF ISSUE	POSITION TAKEN	TYPES OF ACTION SUGGESTED
Uganda	Speech	X	Favors	P (Appeal
United Republic of Tanzania	Speech	X	Favors	P (Appeal)
Upper Volta	Speech	X	Favors	P (Appeal)
Zaire	Speech	X	Favors	P (Appeal)
Zambia	Speech	X	Favors	P (Appeal)

CONTENT ANALYSIS OF THE ISSUE OF THE ECONOMIC DEVELOPMENT FROM THE GENERAL DEBATE SPEECHES OF ALL AFRICAN NATIONS AT THE THIRTIETH SESSION OF THE UNITED NATIONS (1975)

NATION	SPEECHES	FLOOR DISCUSSION OF ISSUE	POSITION TAKEN	TYPES OF ACTION SUGGESTED
Algeria	Speech	X	Favors	NR
Botswana	No Speech			NR
Burundi	No Speech			NR
Cameroon	Speech	X	Favors	P (Appeal)
Central African Republic	No Speech			NR
Chad	Speech	X	Favors	P (Appeal)
Congo	Speech	X	Favors	P (Appeal)
Dahomey	Speech	X	Favors	P (Appeal)
Democartic Republic of Sao TOme & Principe	No Speech			NR
Equatorial Guniea	Speech	X	Favors	P (Appeal)
Ethiopia	No Speech			NR
Gabon	Speech	X	Favors	P (Appeal)
Gambia	No Speech			NR
Ghana	Speech	X	Favors	P (Negotiation)
Guinea	No Speech			NR
Ivory Coast	No Speech			NR
Kenya	Speech	X	Favors	P (Appeal)
Lesotho	Speech	X	Favors	P (Appeal)

2/Economic Development (1975)

NATION	SPEECHES	FLOOR DISCUSSION OF ISSUE	POSITION TAKEN	TYPES OF ACTION SUGGESTED
Liberia	Speech	X	Favors	P (Negotiation)
Libya	Speech	None		NR
Madagascar	Speech	None		NR
Malawi	No Speech			NR
Mali	Speech	X	Favors	P (Negotiation)
Mauritania	Speech	X	Favors	P (Appeal)
Morocco	Speech	X	Favors	P (Appeal)
Niger	No Speech			NR
Nigeria	Speech	X	Favors	P (Appeal)
People's Republic of Congo	No Speech			NR
People's Republic of Mozambique	Speech	X	Favors	P (Appeal
Republic of Cape Verde	No Speech			NR
Rwanda	Speech	X	Favors	P (Appeal)
Senegal	Speech	X	Favors	P (Negotiation)
Sierra Leone	Speech	X	Favors	P (Negotiation)
Somalia	Speech	X	Favors	P (Appeal)
Sudan	Speech	X	Favors	P (Appeal)

3/Economic Development (1975)

NATION	SPEECHES	FLOOR DISCUSSION OF ISSUE	POSITION TAKEN	TYPES OF ACTION SUGGESTED
Swaziland	No Speech			
Togo	Speech	X	Favors	P (Negotiation)
Tunisia	Speech	X	Favors	P (Appeal)
Uganda	Speech	X	Favors	P (Appeal)
United Arab Republic	No Speech			
United Republic of Tanzania	Speech	X	Favors	NR
Upper Volta	Speech	X	Favors	P (Appeal)
Zambia	Speech	X	Favors	P (Negotiation)

248

ABOUT THE AUTHOR:

Gregory L. Wilkins earned his B.A. degree from
Morehouse College in Atlanta, Georgia in 1971. He was
the recipient of a Ford Foundation Fellowship to pursue
graduate studies at the University of Illinois at Urbana
in the Political Science Department, in September, 1971.
He completed all requirements and received the M.A.
degree in 1973 and the Ph.D. in 1979. In the Fall of
1976 he received a National Teaching Fellowship to teach
on the faculty of Shaw College at Detroit, Michigan, where
he is presently on faculty. In 1969, he participated in
Crossroads Africa where he visited and traveled in
West Africa.

DATE DUE
